American
Heart
Association®

BLS for Healthcare Providers

INSTRUCTOR MANUAL

Editor

Mary Fran Hazinski, RN, MSN, *Senior Science Editor*

Senior Managing Editor

S. Lynn Hunter-Wilson

Special Contributors

Janet Butler, MS, *BLS HCP Writer*
Robin R. Hemphill, MD, MPH, *Content Consultant*
Robert A. Berg, MD
Diana M. Cave, RN, MSN
Marc D. Berg, MD
Diana D. Elmore, RN
Michael R. Sayre, MD
Peter A. Meaney, MD, MPH
Louis Gonzales, BS, LP
David Rogers, EdS, NREMT-P

BLS Subcommittee 2010-2011

Robert A. Berg, MD, *Chair*
Diana M. Cave, RN, MSN, *Immediate Past Chair, 2007-2009*
Ben Bobrow, MD
Carolyn L. Cason, RN, PhD
Paul S. Chan, MD, MSc
Todd J. Crocco, MD
Michael Cudnik, MD, MPH
Mohamud Daya, MD, MS
Dana P. Edelson, MD, MS
Barbara Furry, RNC, MS, CCRN
Raúl J. Gazmuri, MD, PhD
Theresa Hoadley, RN, PhD, TNS
Elizabeth A. Hunt, MD, MPH
Victor Johnson, EMT-P
Mary Beth Mancini, RN, PhD
Peter A. Meaney, MD, MPH
James Newcome, NREMT-P
Thomas D. Rea, MD, MPH
Robert Swor, DO
Andrew H. Travers, MD, MSc
Brian Walsh, RRT

© 2011 American Heart Association
ISBN 978-1-61669-040-3
Printed in the United States of America
First American Heart Association Printing March 2011
10 9 8 7 6 5

D0888330

i

BLS Subcommittee 2009-2010

Robert A. Berg, MD, *Chair*

Diana M. Cave, RN, MSN, *Immediate Past Chair, 2007-2009*

Benjamin Abella, MD, MPhil

Tom P. Aufderheide, MD

Ben Bobrow, MD

Richard Branson, MS

Carolyn L. Cason, RN, PhD

Paul S. Chan, MD, MSc

Todd J. Crocco, MD

Michael Cudnik, MD, MPH

Valerie J. De Maio, MD, MSc

Raúl J. Gazmuri, MD, PhD

Ahamed Idris, MD

E. Brooke Lerner, PhD

Peter A. Meaney, MD, MPH

Vincent N. Mosesso, Jr., MD

Thomas D. Rea, MD, MPH

Robert Swor, DO

Andrew H. Travers, MD, MSc

Teresa Ann Volsko, RRT

Pediatric Subcommittee 2010-2011

Marc D. Berg, MD, *Chair*

Monica E. Kleinman, MD, *Immediate Past Chair, 2007-2009*

Dianne L. Atkins, MD

Kathleen Brown, MD

Adam Cheng, MD

Laura Conley, BS, RRT, RCP, NPS

Allan R. de Caen, MD

Aaron Donoghue, MD, MSCE

Melinda L. Fiedor Hamilton, MD, MSc

Ericka L. Fink, MD

Eugene B. Freid, MD

Cheryl K. Gooden, MD

Sharon E. Mace, MD

Bradley S. Marino, MD, MPP, MSCE

Reylon Meeks, RN, BSN, MS, MSN, EMT, PhD

Jeffrey M. Perlman, MB, ChB

Lester Proctor, MD

Faiqa A. Qureshi, MD

Kennith Hans Sartorelli, MD

Wendy Simon, MA

Mark A. Terry, MPA, NREMT-P

Alexis Topjian, MD

Elise W. van der Jagt, MD, MPH

Pediatric Subcommittee 2009-2010

Marc D. Berg, MD, *Chair*

Monica E. Kleinman, MD, *Immediate Past Chair, 2007-2009*

Dianne L. Atkins, MD

Jeffrey M. Berman, MD

Kathleen Brown, MD

Adam Cheng, MD

Laura Conley, BS, RRT, RCP, NPS

Allan R. de Caen, MD

Aaron Donoghue, MD, MSCE

Melinda L. Fiedor Hamilton, MD, MSc

Ericka L. Fink, MD

Eugene B. Freid, MD

Cheryl K. Gooden, MD

John Gosford, BS, EMT-P

Patricia Howard

Kelly Kadlec, MD

Sharon E. Mace, MD

Bradley S. Marino, MD, MPP, MSCE

Reylon Meeks, RN, BSN, MS, MSN, EMT, PhD

Vinay Nadkarni, MD

Jeffrey M. Perlman, MB, ChB

Lester Proctor, MD

Faiqa A. Qureshi, MD

Kennith Hans Sartorelli, MD

Wendy Simon, MA

Mark A. Terry, MPA, NREMT-P

Alexis Topjian, MD

Elise W. van der Jagt, MD, MPH

Arno Zaritsky, MD

To find out about any updates or corrections to this text, visit **www.ahainstructornetwork.org**, navigate to the page for this course, and click on "Updates." You must be registered and confirmed as an Instructor on the AHA Instructor Network to access these updates.

Welcome to the American Heart Association BLS for Healthcare Providers Course. Your instructor materials have 4 major components:

BLS for Healthcare Providers Instructor Manual and CD	The Instructor Manual is the centerpiece of your teaching. It has everything you need to start teaching your BLS for Healthcare Providers Course. When preparing to teach, you should begin with this component.
BLS for Healthcare Providers DVD	Used with the Instructor Manual, the DVD presents content for the BLS for Healthcare Providers Course and Renewal Course.
BLS Instructor Materials Online	Digital copies of forms and checklists to support skills practice and testing for online courses can be found on the AHA Instructor Network in the Courses section. You must be registered and confirmed as an Instructor on the AHA Instructor Network to access these tools. You can access the Instructor Network here: **www.ahainstructornetwork.org**
BLS for Healthcare Providers Student Manual	The Student Manual is provided for your reference, to let you see the information your students are seeing.

BLS for Healthcare Providers Instructor CD

Instructions

The BLS for Healthcare Providers Instructor CD-ROM will auto-launch when the CD is inserted in the drive. If AutoRun has been disabled on your computer, you can right mouse click on the CD drive and choose "Explore" (Windows PC user). Double click on "PC_start.exe" to launch the CD. For the Macintosh user, find and click on "Mac_start.html" to start.

System Requirements

PC

- Pentium 4 550-MHz processor or equivalent AMD processor
- Microsoft Windows 98, Windows NTTM 4.0, Windows 2000, Windows XP Professional or Home Edition, or Windows 7 (all versions)
- 128 MB of RAM (512 MB recommended)
- 250 MB of available hard-disk space
- Internet Explorer 6.0/Mozilla Firefox 1.5.0 Web browser or later
- Screen resolution of 1024 × 768 or higher
- CD-ROM drive (8× or faster)
- Adobe Acrobat Reader 6.0 or later

Mac

- Processor PowerPC iMac, iBook, MacBook, Mac Pro, G3, G4, or faster
- Mac OS 9, OS X, or later
- 128 MB of RAM (512 MB recommended)
- 250 MB of available hard-disk space
- Safari 1.3.2/Mozilla Firefox 2.0.0.1 Web browser or later
- Screen resolution of 1024 × 768 or higher
- CD-ROM drive (8× or faster)
- Adobe Acrobat Reader 6.0 or later

This CD-ROM contains Adobe Acrobat (PDF) and Microsoft Word (DOC) files.

If you do not own Adobe Acrobat, you can download, for free, Adobe Acrobat Reader from Adobe's website:

http://get.adobe.com/reader/

If you have a problem loading or using the CD, make sure your computer system meets the minimum system requirements. If your system meets the requirements and you are still having trouble, log on to **www.heart. org/cprproductsupport** for additional assistance.

Contents

Part 1
Preparing for the Course   1

Course Objectives and Competencies   *1*

Course Goal   1

Learning Objectives   1

Who Can Take the Course   2

Course Prerequisites   2

Educational Design   2

Faculty Needs   *2*

Who Can Teach the Course   2

Lead Instructor   3

Instructor-to-Student Ratio   3

Course Schedules   *3*

Minimum Course Content   3

Renewal Course   4

Changing the Course for Audience-Specific Needs   4

Course Planning Checklist and Timeline   *5*

Sample Precourse Letter to Students   5

Notifying Training Center of Pending Course   6

Useful Websites for Instructors   6

Ordering Materials   6

Securing Tests   6

Room Requirements   7

Sample Floor Plan   7

Course Support Materials   *8*

Instructor Materials   8

Equipment List   9

Using the Student Manual   10

Part 2
Teaching the Course

11

Course Outline *11*

Understanding Icons 11

BLS for Healthcare Providers Classroom Course Outline 13

BLS for Healthcare Providers Renewal Course Outline 16

Using Lesson Maps *19*

Understanding Lesson Maps 19

Using Lesson Maps 20

Part 3
Testing and Remediation

21

Testing for Course Completion *21*

Skills Testing 21

Written Testing 21

Course Completion Requirements 22

Introduction to Skills Tests 22

Using the Skills Testing Sheets and Criteria 22

1- and 2-Rescuer Adult BLS With AED Skills Testing Sheet 23

1- and 2-Rescuer Adult BLS With AED Skills Testing Criteria

and Descriptors 24

1- and 2-Rescuer Infant BLS Skills Testing Sheet 25

1- and 2-Rescuer Infant BLS Skills Testing Criteria and Descriptors ... 26

When to Give Tests 27

Steps for Testing CPR Skills 27

Retesting Students 27

Using a Stopwatch 28

Starting the 1- and 2-Rescuer Adult or Infant BLS Skills Test 28

Remediation *29*

Remediation Lesson 29

After the Course *29*

Program Evaluation 29

Issuing Cards 29

Part 4
Additional Resources

31

Self-Directed Learning Courses **31**
    BLS for Healthcare Providers Online Courses 31

Additional AHA Courses **32**
    Courses That a BLS Instructor Can Teach 32
    Advanced Cardiovascular Life Support/
        Pediatric Advanced Life Support Courses 32

Recruiting and Mentoring New Instructors **32**
    Recruiting and Mentoring Instructors 32
    Instructor Candidate Selection 32
    Instructor Course Prerequisites 32

Science Update Information **32**
    Update on *2010 AHA Guidelines for CPR and ECC* 32

Part 5
BLS for Healthcare Providers
Lesson Maps
BLS HCP 1-50

Part 6
BLS for Healthcare Providers
Renewal Lesson Maps
BLS HCP Renewal 1-42

BLS for Healthcare Providers
Instructor CD

Precourse Materials

Equipment List

Sample Precourse Letter

Course Materials

1- and 2-Rescuer Adult BLS With AED Skills Testing Sheet

Skills Testing Criteria and Descriptors

1- and 2-Rescuer Infant BLS Skills Testing Sheet

Skills Testing Criteria and Descriptors

Lesson Maps

Renewal Lesson Maps

Other Resources

Emergency Cardiovascular Care Websites for Instructors

Healthcare Provider Summary of Steps of CPR for Adults,
Children, and Infants

Instructor Candidate Application

BLS for Healthcare Providers Video Chapters and
Corresponding Lesson Maps for Full Course

Preparing for the Course

Course Objectives and Competencies

Course Goal

The goal of the BLS for Healthcare Providers Course is to train participants to **save lives** of victims in cardiac arrest through **high-quality cardiopulmonary resuscitation (CPR)**. The American Heart Association designed the BLS for Healthcare Providers Course to prepare healthcare professionals to know how to perform CPR in both in- and out-of-hospital settings. This course trains participants to promptly recognize cardiac arrest, give high-quality chest compressions, deliver appropriate ventilations, and provide early use of an automated external defibrillator (AED), as part of a team and individually. This course also teaches how to relieve choking. The course includes adult, child, and infant rescue techniques.

Learning Objectives

At the end of the BLS for Healthcare Providers Course, students will be able to

1. Initiate the Chain of Survival
   a. Promptly recognize cardiac arrest within 10 seconds
   b. Overcome barriers to initiating CPR

2. Perform prompt, high-quality CPR with C-A-B sequence (adult/child/infant)
   a. Provide chest compressions of adequate rate (at least 100/min)
   b. Provide chest compressions of adequate depth
      i. A depth of at least 2 inches (5 cm) for adults
      ii. A depth of least one third the anterior-posterior diameter of the chest or approximately 1½ inches (4 cm) in infants and 2 inches (5 cm) in children
   c. Allow complete chest recoil after each compression
   d. Minimize interruptions in compressions
   e. Avoid excessive ventilation

3. Initiate early use of an AED (adult/child/infant)
   a. Turn on AED
   b. Place AED pads appropriately
   c. Follow all AED prompts

(continued)

4. Provide appropriate breaths
   a. Deliver appropriate breaths with minimal interruptions in compressions:
      i. 30:2 for an adult, child, or infant without an advanced airway
      ii. 15:2 for 2-rescuer CPR for a child or infant without an advanced airway
      iii. One breath every 6 to 8 seconds (8 to 10 breaths per minute) for a victim with an advanced airway (without pauses in chest compressions)
   b. Provide visible chest rise with each breath
   c. Avoid excessive ventilation

5. Practice the minor basic life support (BLS) differences for children and infants

6. Practice team CPR (adult/infant)
   a. Practice team resuscitation to optimize coordinated CPR to achieve objectives 1 through 4
   b. Change rescuers every 2 minutes to avoid compressor fatigue
   c. Provide constructive feedback to other team members

Who Can Take the Course

This course focuses on students who provide health care to patients in a wide variety of settings, including in-hospital and out-of-hospital settings. Anyone who needs to know how to perform CPR in a healthcare setting can take this course. Rescuers who want to learn more about performing 1- or 2-rescuer CPR for adult, child, and infant victims can also take this course.

Course Prerequisites

The BLS for Healthcare Providers Course has no specific prerequisites.

Educational Design

The BLS for Healthcare Providers Course is available in 3 different course formats to best meet the learning needs of the individual student. The course designs include a traditional format, led by an instructor in a classroom setting; computer-based learning with automated manikin practice; and eLearning with instructor-led practice and skills verification.

The BLS for Healthcare Providers Course uses video to guide practice. Studies show that students who practice CPR with a training video to guide their practice learn and retain the skills much better than in other learning models.

The instructor is a key element in the classroom-based course. The course structure ensures that instructors can focus attention on observing students carefully, giving feedback, and guiding students' acquisition of skills. The ultimate goal is that the student can perform the BLS skills to save a life upon exiting the course.

Although video instruction provides the framework for the BLS for Healthcare Providers Course, the instructor helps coach the students and facilitate every traditional classroom-based BLS course.

Faculty Needs

Who Can Teach the Course

Any current AHA BLS Instructor may teach the BLS for Healthcare Providers Course. BLS Faculty at the Training Center, regional, and national levels are qualified to teach as well.

Lead Instructor

If more than 1 instructor will teach the course, designate a lead instructor. The lead instructor will oversee the communication among all instructors before and during the course. The lead instructor will also be responsible for issuing and ensuring that students receive course completion cards from the instructor's Training Center.

Instructor-to-Student Ratio

The course size for the BLS for Healthcare Providers Course is flexible, and there is currently no research-based best instructor-to-student ratio. However, the course is designed to use a ratio of 3 students to 1 manikin. With this ratio, 1 instructor observes 2 students during video-led manikin practice (practice-while-watching). Each video segment repeats up to 3 times to allow all students a chance to practice.

Experienced instructors may monitor up to 3 manikin stations at a time while the students practice. This would change the ratio to 9 students to 3 manikins to 1 instructor. However, for each student over the ideal number of 6 students per instructor, the total class time will increase by approximately 18 minutes to allow for individual skills testing. The following table shows how the number of students per instructor affects the additional course time.

Number of Students	Number of Manikins	Additional Course Time Required
6	2	0
7	3	18 minutes
8	3	36 minutes
9	3	54 minutes

For optimal practice time during the course, each student would have his own manikin if possible. But using a 1:1 student-to-manikin ratio will *not* decrease overall class time. One instructor cannot adequately monitor more than 3 manikin stations during a single practice-while-watching video segment.

For skills testing, use a 1:2 instructor-to-student ratio.

Course Schedules

Minimum Course Content

The BLS for Healthcare Providers Course includes these components:

- Part 1: General Concepts
- Part 2: BLS/CPR for Adults
- Part 3: Automated External Defibrillator for Adults and for Children 8 Years of Age and Older
- Part 4: BLS/CPR for Children From 1 Year of Age to Puberty
- Part 5: BLS/CPR for Infants
- Part 6: Automated External Defibrillator for Infants and for Children From 1 to 8 Years of Age
- Part 7: CPR With an Advanced Airway
- Part 8: Mouth-to-Mouth Breaths
- Part 9: Rescue Breathing
- Part 10: Relief of Choking

Renewal Course

Classroom-Based Renewal

Because of science changes and the consequent changes in the *2010 AHA Guidelines for CPR and ECC,* through March 31, 2013, all students in the classroom-based course must watch the BLS for Healthcare Providers Renewal video and practice with the video before taking the skills test and written test. After the initial 2-year period has ended, instructors can continue to choose to use the renewal video for the classroom-based course or just perform a skills test and written exam.

Online Renewal

- Students can also take a renewal course online by completing BLS for Healthcare Providers Online Part 1 or HeartCode® BLS Part 1. Students can enroll at **OnlineAHA.org.**

Note: With either method students must pass the BLS for Healthcare Providers skills test with a BLS Instructor or with the use of a voice-assisted manikin (VAM) system.

Recommended Renewal Timeline

Numerous evaluations of CPR and AED training courses confirm that skills performance begins to decline within months, even days, of initial training. After training in CPR, students need *refresher, retention,* or *renewal* training. Students should read their manuals periodically and practice whenever possible to refresh their knowledge and should also take advantage of any opportunity to practice their CPR and AED skills frequently during the 2 years after this course.

The recommended 2-year interval represents the current administrative requirement. Research, however, has not yet identified the optimal renewal interval to ensure maximal preparation for performing CPR.

Changing the Course for Audience-Specific Needs

The AHA allows instructors to tailor the classroom-based BLS for Healthcare Providers Course to meet audience-specific needs. For example, if you are giving this course to staff at a children's hospital, you might want to have extra practice time on infant manikins. Any changes to the course are in addition to the basic course contents outlined above and will add to the length of the course. Instructors may not delete course lessons or course components. Any additions or alterations to the course must be specifically identified as non-AHA material.

Addressing audience-specific needs would also mean the ability to adapt situations to specific locations, eliminate "call 911" for students who are emergency medical services responders, and so on.

Course Planning Checklist and Timeline

Sample Precourse Letter to Students

The letter below is a sample you may modify and send to students attending a classroom-based course.

(Date)

Dear BLS for Healthcare Providers Course Student:

Welcome to the BLS for Healthcare Providers Course. Enclosed are the agenda and your copy of the *BLS for Healthcare Providers Student Manual* to help you prepare for the program and the written exam. Review both before coming to class; you will learn more and will be more comfortable with the course.

The class will be

Date: _____

Time: _____

Location: _____

What to Expect

Please wear loose, comfortable clothing. You will be practicing skills that require working on your hands and knees, bending, standing, and lifting. If you have physical conditions that might prevent you from participating in the course, please tell one of the instructors when you arrive for the course. The instructor will work to accommodate your needs within the stated course completion requirements.

We look forward to welcoming you on _____. If you have any questions about the course, please call
_____ at _____.

Sincerely,

Program Coordinator
(Day of class)
(Name) (Telephone number)

Notifying Training Center of Pending Course

Training Centers that offer classes open to the public should use the AHA's ECC Class Connector online tool to list their Training Center profile and/or classes scheduled. Customers then are able to access this information through the online tool or by phone at 1-877-AHA-4CPR (1-877-242-4277).

Training Center profile information is entered through the Training Center Coordinator's access to the AHA Instructor Network. Scheduled classes can be entered through the AHA Instructor Network by either Training Center Coordinators or instructors; however, instructors should check with their Training Center Coordinator for any rules or restrictions the Training Center has established about instructors entering their classes.

All Training Center Coordinators receive automatic access to the AHA Instructor Network. Instructors must register with the AHA Instructor Network and be confirmed by their Training Center Coordinator for access.

Many Training Centers also have websites on which they post information about their courses.

Useful Websites for Instructors

The AHA provides these websites for instructors:

- ECC Class Connector: **www.heart.org/eccclassconnector**
- AHA Instructor Network: **www.ahainstructornetwork.org**

Ordering Materials

To help in the distribution of emergency cardiovascular care (ECC) materials, AHA has partnered with several companies that provide high-quality customer service and support. To order materials, contact one of these companies, listed on the back of this manual.

Instructors can directly order books or support materials from any of the AHA distributors. Only a Training Center Coordinator can order cards. However, it is ultimately the BLS Instructor's responsibility to ensure that students receive their course completion cards.

Securing Tests

The Customer Support Center provides all Training Center Coordinators with copies of the current written tests for AHA course completion when released by the National Center ECC Department. To prevent possible compromise of the test contents, the AHA issues tests only to Training Center Coordinators.

Test security is of the utmost importance. Training Centers and instructors should ensure that all written tests are secure and not copied or distributed outside the classroom.

Use the most current tests to determine successful course completion.

Room Requirements

You can teach an average course of 12 students with 2 instructors in 1 large room. The room must comfortably accommodate at least 20 people. There should be an open space at the front of the classroom for practice with chairs around the manikins, a manikin practice area where the students can see the video screen or TV, and seating space for written tests and other course activities. Instructors must ensure that all students have an unobstructed view of the video screen while kneeling at the manikin for practice.

The room should have

- Good acoustics
- Good lighting that can be dimmed or adjusted for video presentations
- An instructor-controlled video player and monitor large enough to be viewed by all course students. (Although a TV may be acceptable for small classes with only a few groups, larger classes with several manikins may require a large-screen TV or an LCD projector.)
- Table and chairs for the written test
- Optimally, a separate room for the written test
- Ideally, a firm surface with adequate padding/protection for skills practice (eg, carpeted floors or padded mats)
- A chair for each student

Sample Floor Plan

The following picture shows a sample floor plan.

Screen

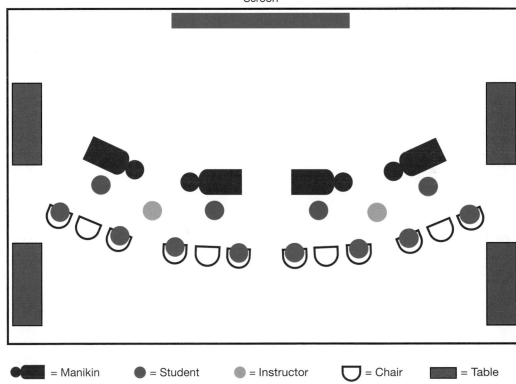

● = Manikin   ● = Student   ● = Instructor   ⊔ = Chair   ▬ = Table

Course Support Materials

Instructor Materials

Instructor materials for classroom-based courses and skills evaluations include the following:

Item	Description	Use
BLS for Healthcare Providers Student Manual	Textbook with review questions	• Require students to read it before coming to class. • Tell students to bring it to class and follow along during class. • Tell students to refer to it after the course to maintain knowledge.
BLS for Healthcare Providers Online Part 1	Self-directed eLearning	• Students complete Part 1 online, Part 2 is the practice session, and Part 3 is the skills evaluation. Part 2 allows the students to practice the physical skills they learned online, to ask questions, and to receive coaching from the BLS Instructor. Part 3 is skills testing with the BLS Instructor.
HeartCode BLS Part 1	Self-directed eLearning	• Students complete Part 1 online; Part 2 is the practice session and skills evaluation. Part 2 allows the students to practice the physical skills they learned online, to ask questions, and to receive coaching from the VAM system or BLS Instructor. Part 3 is skills testing with the VAM system or BLS Instructor.
***BLS for Healthcare Providers* video**	DVD • Approximately 2 hours in duration • Practice-while-watching format	• Tell students to practice while watching the video.
Skills Testing Sheet reproduction masters	Two 2-sided sheets with checklists: • 1- and 2-Rescuer Adult CPR and AED • 1- and 2-Rescuer Infant CPR	• Use these to check the student's actions during the skills tests.

(continued)

(continued)

Item	Description	Use
Lesson Maps	Cards with information about what each lesson includes	• Review these before class to understand your role and the necessary equipment. • Refer to these during the course to know what each lesson includes and what you need to do to help students meet their learning objectives for each lesson.
2010 Handbook of Emergency Cardiovascular Care for Healthcare Providers	Quick reference containing all algorithms and many key tables from the *2010 AHA Guidelines for CPR and ECC* and training materials	• Use this for more details on BLS and CPR.
Highlights of the 2010 AHA Guidelines for CPR and ECC	Summary of changes in the *2010 AHA Guidelines for CPR and ECC*	• Use this for more details on BLS and CPR.

Equipment List

The following table lists the required equipment for the BLS for Healthcare Providers Course and skills testing:

Quantity	Equipment
1 per student	Student Manual (classroom-based student)
	Two versions of tests (classroom-based student)
	Blank test answer sheets (classroom-based student)
	One-way valve
	Course completion card
	Pencil or pen
	Course agenda
	Skills Testing Sheets
	Course evaluation
1 per set of 3 students (3:1 student-to-manikin ratio)	AED trainer with adult pads
	Manikins (adult/child, infant) (child manikin is optional)
	Pocket mask
	Bag-mask (appropriate sizes for each manikin used)
	Stopwatch

(continued)

(continued)

Quantity	Equipment
1 per course	TV with DVD player or Laptop or PC with projector, screen, and speakers
	Course DVD
	Test answer key
	Course roster
	Instructor Manual with Lesson Maps
	Manikin cleaning supplies (such as alcohol pads)

Using the Student Manual

The AHA designed the Student Manual to correspond with the video. The Lesson Maps tell you when to refer students to specific pages in the manual. Encourage students to follow along in their manuals while the video is running.

eLearning students have access to the Student Manual and other reference materials through the **OnlineAHA.org** website. Students have access to the reference materials for 2 years from the key activation date.

Part **2**

Teaching the Course

Course Outline

Understanding Icons

The Lesson Maps and video use these icons to remind you to take certain actions during the course. This approach recognizes that the busy instructor may not be able to keep track of or remember every important action to take.

These icons signal what to do throughout the course:

Icon	Action
▶	Show the video/play the video
❚❚	Pause the video
■	Stop the video

(continued)

(continued)

Icon	Action
PWW	Students practice while watching the video
	Students practice after watching the video
	Discussion
T	Test

BLS for Healthcare Providers Classroom Course Outline

Approximate course duration: 4½ hours

Student-instructor ratio 6:1; student-manikin ratio 3:1

Lesson Map	Course Event	Time Estimate (in minutes)
HCP 1	Course Introduction	👤👤 5
HCP 2	Course Overview and *2010 AHA Guidelines for CPR and ECC* Science Update	▶ 12
HCP 3	BLS/CPR Basics for Adults	▶ 1
HCP 4	1-Rescuer CPR With AED Demo	▶ 1
HCP 5	Assessment and Scene Safety	▶ 1
HCP 6	Chest Compressions for Adult Victims	PWW 8
HCP 7	Airway and Breathing	PWW 6
HCP 8	Adult Compressions and Breaths Practice	PWW 8
HCP 9	1-Rescuer Adult BLS Practice Session	▶ PWW 12
HCP 10	Breaths With Bag-Mask for Adult Victims	PWW 12
HCP 11	2-Rescuer Adult BLS/Team CPR Sequence	▶ 3
HCP 12	Defibrillation: AED Introduction and Use	▶ 3

Lesson Map	Course Event	Time Estimate (in minutes)
HCP 13	AED Special Situations and Safety	▶ 2
HCP 14	Using the AED Trainer	👥 4
HCP 15	1- and 2-Rescuer Adult BLS With AED Practice Session	▶ 🧑‍⚕️ 25
HCP 16	Introduction to Child BLS/CPR	▶ 2
HCP 17	Chest Compressions for Child Victims	**PWW** 5
HCP 18	Introduction to Infant BLS/CPR	▶ 1
HCP 19	1- and 2-Rescuer Infant BLS/CPR Demo	▶ 2
HCP 20	2-Finger Chest Compressions for Infant Victims	**PWW** 7
HCP 21	Breaths With Bag-Mask for Infant Victims	**PWW** 4
HCP 22	2-Rescuer Infant CPR/2 Thumb–Encircling Hands Chest Compressions for Infant Victims	**PWW** 8
HCP 23	1- and 2-Rescuer Infant BLS/CPR Practice Session	▶ 🧑‍⚕️ 11
HCP 24	AED for Infants and Children From 1 to 8 Years of Age	▶ 2
HCP 25	CPR With an Advanced Airway	▶ 1

Lesson Map	Course Event	Time Estimate (in minutes)
HCP 26	Rescue Breathing	▶ 4
HCP 27	Mouth-to-Mouth Breaths for Victims 1 Year of Age and Older	▶ 1
HCP 28	Adult/Child Choking (Responsive)	▶ ‖ OPTIONAL 2
HCP 29	Adult/Child Choking (Unresponsive)	▶ 1
HCP 30	Infant Choking (Responsive)	PWW 6
HCP 31	Infant Choking (Unresponsive)	▶ 1
HCP 32	Course Summary and Closure	▶ 1
HCP 33	Written Test	T 25
HCP 34	1- and 2-Rescuer Adult BLS With AED Skills Test	T 30
HCP 35	1- and 2-Rescuer Infant BLS Skills Test	T 30
HCP 36	Remediation	T Variable

BLS for Healthcare Providers Renewal Course Outline

Approximate course duration: 4 hours
Student-instructor ratio 6:1; student-manikin ratio 3:1

Lesson Map	Course Event	Time Estimate (in minutes)
HCP-R 1	Course Introduction	5
HCP-R 2	Course Overview and *2010 AHA Guidelines for CPR and ECC* Science Update	12
HCP-R 3	BLS/CPR Basics for Adults	1
HCP-R 4	2-Rescuer CPR With AED Demo	1
HCP-R 5	Assessment and Scene Safety	1
HCP-R 6	Chest Compressions for Adult Victims	PWW 8
HCP-R 7	Airway and Breathing	PWW 6
HCP-R 8	Breaths With Bag-Mask for Adult Victims	PWW 8
HCP-R 9	Adult Compressions and Breaths Practice	PWW 8
HCP-R 10	2-Rescuer Adult BLS/Team CPR Sequence	3

Lesson Map	Course Event	Time Estimate (in minutes)
HCP-R 11	Defibrillation: AED Introduction and Use	▶ 3
HCP-R 12	Using the AED Trainer	👥 4
HCP-R 13	1- and 2-Rescuer Adult BLS With AED Practice Session	▶ 🧑 16
HCP-R 14	Introduction to Child BLS/CPR	▶ 2
HCP-R 15	Chest Compressions for Child Victims	PWW 3
HCP-R 16	Introduction to Infant BLS/CPR	▶ 3
HCP-R 17	1- and 2-Rescuer Infant BLS/CPR Demo	▶ 3
HCP-R 18	1- and 2-Rescuer Infant BLS/CPR Practice Session	▶ 🧑 10
HCP-R 19	AED for Infants and Children From 1 to 8 Years of Age	▶ 1
HCP-R 20	CPR With an Advanced Airway	▶ 1
HCP-R 21	Rescue Breathing	▶ 1

Lesson Map	Course Event	Time Estimate (in minutes)
HCP-R 22	Mouth-to-Mouth Breaths for Victims 1 Year of Age and Older	▶ 1
HCP-R 23	Adult/Child Choking (Responsive)	▶ OPTIONAL ❚❚ 1
HCP-R 24	Adult/Child Choking (Unresponsive)	▶ 1
HCP-R 25	Infant Choking (Responsive)	PWW 6
HCP-R 26	Infant Choking (Unresponsive)	▶ 1
HCP-R 27	Course Summary and Closure	▶ 2
HCP-R 28	Written Test	T 25
HCP-R 29	1- and 2-Rescuer Adult BLS With AED Skills Test	T 30
HCP-R 30	1- and 2-Rescuer Infant BLS Skills Test	T 30
HCP-R 31	Remediation	T Variable

Using Lesson Maps

Understanding Lesson Maps

The AHA instructor materials include Lesson Maps to help you better facilitate courses. The Lesson Maps help ensure consistency from course to course and help keep the instructor focused on the main objectives for each lesson. Lesson Maps are for instructor use only.

Each Lesson Map represents the main components for that lesson:

- Course identifier
- Lesson number
- Major topics
- Icon for type of lesson
- Reference to Student Manual
- Resources needed
- Student role
- Student objectives
- Instructor role
- Duration (in minutes)

The following graphic is a sample Lesson Map:

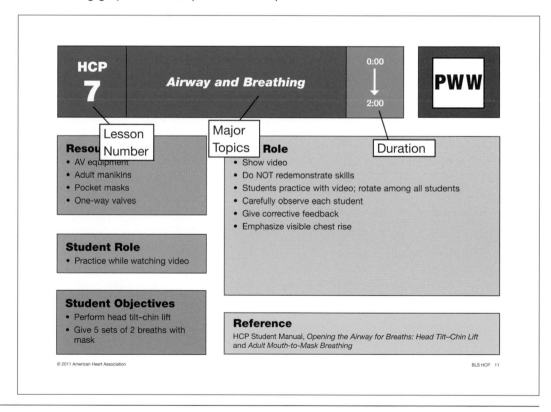

Using Lesson Maps

There are many ways to use these Lesson Maps:

When	Then you can:
Before the course	Review the maps to understand • The objectives for each lesson. • Your role for each Lesson Map. • The resources that you need for each lesson.
During the course	Follow each Lesson Map as you conduct the course. • Remind students what they will see in each video segment. • Make sure you have all resources ready for each lesson. • Help the students achieve the objectives identified for each lesson.
During practice before a skills evaluation (Part 2 for online students)	A student may have a question about a certain part of CPR. The Lesson Maps serve as the authoritative answer.

Part 3

Testing and Remediation

Testing for Course Completion

Skills Testing

The AHA CPR courses are designed to increase learning of CPR skills by providing more skills practice time through

- Enhanced video practice
- More instructor feedback during skills practice

As part of this emphasis on better teaching and learning, the AHA developed CPR skills tests to ensure that instructors use a more uniform and objective approach for testing CPR skills. These skills tests include skills testing sheets that help instructors evaluate each student's CPR skills. As a result of the course design and skills tests, the AHA expects that students in CPR classes will learn more effectively and instructors will work with students to achieve higher levels of CPR skills competency.

CPR competency is critical to victim survival. It is important that you use the skills testing sheets to evaluate each student's performance and to ensure consistent testing and learning across all AHA BLS for Healthcare Providers courses. Your adherence to these testing procedures will enhance the CPR competency of your students. Retain student skills testing sheets per the *Program Administration Manual* or Training Center policy.

Important: After practice, students must demonstrate competency without any assistance, hints, or prompting.

Written Testing

The written test measures the mastery of cognitive skills. Each student must take the written test without using the Student Manual or any other resource for help. This is to be a closed-book test.

In some self-directed learning courses, the written test is included in the software program according to the policy for that individual course. Students can print a certificate upon successful completion of Part 1 of the course.

Instructors may read the test to a student who has a learning disability or language barrier.

Each student must score at least 84% on the written test.

Course Completion Requirements

To receive a course completion card, students in the BLS for Healthcare Providers Course must pass both BLS skills tests and a written test by doing the following:

Skills Test Requirements	Written Test Requirements
Students must successfully pass these skills tests by being evaluated once in each role: • 1- and 2-Rescuer Adult BLS With AED • 1- and 2-Rescuer Infant BLS	Score at least 84% on the written test

Introduction to Skills Tests

Over the past few years, educational research has shown that people who take CPR classes often are unable to perform CPR well, even immediately after a CPR class. Studies have shown that students do not retain CPR skills even just a few weeks after taking a CPR class.

Early CPR is an important factor in the effectiveness of defibrillation and subsequent patient survival. Victims who receive high-quality CPR are more likely to survive.

Using the Skills Testing Sheets and Criteria

Use the skills descriptions in the skills testing sheet criteria to determine if a student has demonstrated each step of the skill correctly and to record the student's results.

- If the student successfully completes a step, place a check (✓) in the box to the right of the step.
- If the student is unsuccessful, leave the box to the right of the step blank and circle the step under the critical performance criteria that the student did not complete successfully.

If a student demonstrates each step of the skill successfully, mark the student as passing that skill test. If a student does not pass a skills test, refer the student to the Remediation lesson at the end of the course for further testing in that skill.

You should be very familiar with each of the descriptions to be able to test BLS skills correctly.

BLS for Healthcare Providers Course
1- and 2-Rescuer Adult BLS With AED Skills Testing Sheet

See 1- and 2-Rescuer Adult BLS With AED Skills Testing Criteria and Descriptors on next page

Student Name: _____ Test Date: _____

CPR Skills (circle one):	Pass	Needs Remediation
AED Skills (circle one):	Pass	Needs Remediation

Skill Step	Critical Performance Criteria	✓ if done correctly	
1-Rescuer Adult BLS Skills Evaluation During this first phase, evaluate the first rescuer's ability to initiate BLS and deliver high-quality CPR for 5 cycles.			
1	ASSESSES: Checks for response and for no breathing or no normal breathing, only gasping (at least 5 seconds but no more than 10 seconds)		
2	ACTIVATES emergency response system		
3	Checks for PULSE (no more than 10 seconds)		
4	GIVES HIGH-QUALITY CPR:		
	• Correct compression HAND PLACEMENT	Cycle 1:	
	• ADEQUATE RATE: At least 100/min (ie, delivers each set of 30 chest compressions in 18 seconds or less)	Cycle 2:	Time:
	• ADEQUATE DEPTH: Delivers compressions at least 2 inches in depth (at least 23 out of 30)	Cycle 3:	
	• ALLOWS COMPLETE CHEST RECOIL (at least 23 out of 30)	Cycle 4:	
	• MINIMIZES INTERRUPTIONS: Gives 2 breaths with pocket mask in less than 10 seconds	Cycle 5:	
Second Rescuer AED Skills Evaluation and SWITCH During this next phase, evaluate the second rescuer's ability to use the AED and both rescuers' abilities to switch roles.			
5	DURING FIFTH SET OF COMPRESSIONS: Second rescuer arrives with AED and bag-mask device, turns on AED, and applies pads		
6	First rescuer continues compressions while second rescuer turns on AED and applies pads		
7	Second rescuer clears victim, allowing AED to analyze—RESCUERS SWITCH		
8	If AED indicates a shockable rhythm, second rescuer clears victim again and delivers shock		
First Rescuer Bag-Mask Ventilation During this next phase, evaluate the first rescuer's ability to give breaths with a bag-mask.			
9	Both rescuers RESUME HIGH-QUALITY CPR immediately after shock delivery:	Cycle 1	Cycle 2
	• SECOND RESCUER gives 30 compressions immediately after shock delivery (for 2 cycles)		
	• FIRST RESCUER successfully delivers 2 breaths with bag-mask (for 2 cycles)		
AFTER 2 CYCLES, STOP THE EVALUATION			

- If the student completes all steps successfully (a ✓ in each box to the right of Critical Performance Criteria), the student passed this scenario.
- If the student does not complete all steps successfully (as indicated by a blank box to the right of any of the Critical Performance Criteria), give the form to the student for review as part of the student's remediation.
- After reviewing the form, the student will give the form to the instructor who is reevaluating the student. The student will reperform the entire scenario, and the instructor will notate the reevaluation on this same form.
- If the reevaluation is to be done at a different time, the instructor should collect this sheet before the student leaves the classroom.

	Remediation (if needed):
Instructor Signature: _____	Instructor Signature: _____
Print Instructor Name: _____	Print Instructor Name: _____
Date: _____	Date: _____

BLS for Healthcare Providers Course
1- and 2-Rescuer Adult BLS With AED Skills Testing Criteria and Descriptors

1. **Assesses victim (Steps 1 and 2, assessment and activation, must be completed within 10 seconds of arrival at scene):**
   - Checks for unresponsiveness (this MUST precede starting compressions)
   - Checks for no breathing or no normal breathing (only gasping)

2. **Activates emergency response system (Steps 1 and 2, assessment and activation, must be completed within 10 seconds of arrival at scene):**
   - Shouts for help/directs someone to call for help AND get AED/defibrillator

3. **Checks for pulse:**
   - Checks carotid pulse
   - This should take no more than 10 seconds

4. **Delivers high-quality CPR (initiates compressions within 10 seconds of identifying cardiac arrest):**
   - Correct placement of hands/fingers in center of chest
     - Adult: Lower half of breastbone
     - Adult: 2-handed (second hand on top of the first or grasping the wrist of the first hand)
   - Compression rate of at least 100/min
     - Delivers 30 compressions in 18 seconds or less
   - Adequate depth for age
   - Adult: at least 2 inches (5 cm)
   - Complete chest recoil after each compression
   - Minimizes interruptions in compressions:
     - Less than 10 seconds between last compression of one cycle and first compression of next cycle
     - Compressions not interrupted until AED analyzing rhythm
     - Compressions resumed immediately after shock/no shock indicated

5-8. **Integrates prompt and proper use of AED with CPR:**
   - Turns AED on
   - Places proper-sized pads for victim's age in correct location
   - Clears rescuers from victim for AED to analyze rhythm (pushes ANALYZE button if required by device)
   - Clears victim and delivers shock
   - Resumes chest compressions immediately after shock delivery
   - Does NOT turn off AED during CPR
   - Provides safe environment for rescuers during AED shock delivery:
     - Communicates clearly to all other rescuers to stop touching victim
     - Delivers shock to victim after all rescuers are clear of victim
   - Switches during analysis phase of AED

9. **Provides effective breaths:**
   - Opens airway adequately
   - Delivers each breath over 1 second
   - Delivers breaths that produce visible chest rise
   - Avoids excessive ventilation

BLS for Healthcare Providers Course
1- and 2-Rescuer Infant BLS
Skills Testing Sheet

See 1- and 2-Rescuer Infant BLS Skills Testing Criteria and Descriptors on next page

American Heart Association®

Student Name: _____ Test Date: _____

1-Rescuer BLS and CPR Skills (circle one):	Pass	Needs Remediation
2-Rescuer CPR Skills		
Bag-Mask (circle one):	Pass	Needs Remediation
2 Thumb–Encircling Hands (circle one):	Pass	Needs Remediation

Skill Step	Critical Performance Criteria	✓ if done correctly	
1-Rescuer Infant BLS Skills Evaluation			
During this first phase, evaluate the first rescuer's ability to initiate BLS and deliver high-quality CPR for 5 cycles.			
1	ASSESSES: Checks for response and for no breathing or only gasping (at least 5 seconds but no more than 10 seconds)		
2	Sends someone to ACTIVATE emergency response system		
3	Checks for PULSE (no more than 10 seconds)		
4	GIVES HIGH-QUALITY CPR:		
	• Correct compression FINGER PLACEMENT	Cycle 1:	
	• ADEQUATE RATE: At least 100/min (ie, delivers each set of 30 chest compressions in 18 seconds or less)	Cycle 2:	Time:
	• ADEQUATE DEPTH: Delivers compressions at least one third the depth of the chest (approximately 1½ inches [4 cm]) (at least 23 out of 30)	Cycle 3:	
	• ALLOWS COMPLETE CHEST RECOIL (at least 23 out of 30)	Cycle 4:	
	• MINIMIZES INTERRUPTIONS: Gives 2 breaths with pocket mask in less than 10 seconds	Cycle 5:	
2-Rescuer CPR and SWITCH			
During this next phase, evaluate the FIRST RESCUER'S ability to give breaths with a bag-mask and give compressions by using the 2 thumb–encircling hands technique. Also evaluate both rescuers' abilities to switch roles.			
5	DURING FIFTH SET OF COMPRESSIONS: Second rescuer arrives with bag-mask device. RESCUERS SWITCH ROLES.		
6	Both rescuers RESUME HIGH-QUALITY CPR:	Cycle 1	Cycle 2
	• SECOND RESCUER gives 15 compressions in 9 seconds or less by using 2 thumb–encircling hands technique (for 2 cycles)	X	X
	• FIRST RESCUER successfully delivers 2 breaths with bag-mask (for 2 cycles)		
AFTER 2 CYCLES, PROMPT RESCUERS TO SWITCH ROLES			
7	Both rescuers RESUME HIGH-QUALITY CPR:	Cycle 1	Cycle 2
	• FIRST RESCUER gives 15 compressions in 9 seconds or less by using 2 thumb–encircling hands technique (for 2 cycles)	Time:	Time:
	• SECOND RESCUER successfully delivers 2 breaths with bag-mask (for 2 cycles)	X	X
AFTER 2 CYCLES, STOP THE EVALUATION			

- If the student completes all steps successfully (a ✓ in each box to the right of Critical Performance Criteria), the student passed this scenario.
- If the student does not complete all steps successfully (as indicated by a blank box to the right of any of the Critical Performance Criteria), give the form to the student for review as part of the student's remediation.
- After reviewing the form, the student will give the form to the instructor who is reevaluating the student. The student will reperform the entire scenario, and the instructor will notate the reevaluation on this same form.
- If the reevaluation is to be done at a different time, the instructor should collect this sheet before the student leaves the classroom.

	Remediation (if needed):
Instructor Signature: _____	Instructor Signature: _____
Print Instructor Name: _____	Print Instructor Name: _____
Date: _____	Date: _____

BLS for Healthcare Providers Course
1- and 2-Rescuer Infant BLS
Skills Testing Criteria and Descriptors

1. **Assesses victim (Steps 1 and 2, assessment and activation, must be completed within 10 seconds of arrival at scene):**
   - Checks for unresponsiveness (this MUST precede starting compressions)
   - Checks for no breathing or only gasping

2. **Sends someone to activate emergency response system (Steps 1 and 2, assessment and activation, must be completed within 10 seconds of arrival at scene):**
   - Shouts for help/directs someone to call for help AND get AED/defibrillator
   - If alone, remains with infant to provide 2 minutes of CPR before activating emergency response system

3. **Checks for pulse:**
   - Checks brachial pulse
   - This should take no more than 10 seconds

4. **Delivers high-quality 1-rescuer CPR (initiates compressions within 10 seconds of identifying cardiac arrest):**
   - Correct placement of hands/fingers in center of chest
     - 1 rescuer: 2 fingers just below the nipple line
   - Compression rate of at least 100/min
     - Delivers 30 compressions in 18 seconds or less
   - Adequate depth for age
     - Infant: at least one third the depth of the chest (approximately 1½ inches [4 cm])
   - Complete chest recoil after each compression
   - Appropriate ratio for age and number of rescuers
     - 1 rescuer: 30 compressions to 2 breaths
   - Minimizes interruptions in compressions:
     - Less than 10 seconds between last compression of one cycle and first compression of next cycle

5. **Switches at appropriate intervals as prompted by the instructor (for purposes of this evaluation)**

6. **Provides effective breaths with bag-mask device during 2-rescuer CPR:**
   - Provides effective breaths:
     - Opens airway adequately
     - Delivers each breath over 1 second
     - Delivers breaths that produce visible chest rise
     - Avoids excessive ventilation

7. **Provides high-quality chest compressions during 2-rescuer CPR:**
   - Correct placement of hands/fingers in center of chest
     - 2 rescuers: 2 thumb–encircling hands just below the nipple line
   - Compression rate of at least 100/min
     - Delivers 15 compressions in 9 seconds or less
   - Adequate depth for age
     - Infant: at least one third the depth of the chest (approximately 1½ inches [4 cm])
   - Complete chest recoil after each compression
   - Appropriate ratio for age and number of rescuers
     - 2 rescuers: 15 compressions to 2 breaths
   - Minimizes interruptions in compressions:
     - Less than 10 seconds between last compression of one cycle and first compression of next cycle

When to Give Tests

You will test students

- At the end of the course
- During the testing session (Part 3) for online students completing a skills evaluation

At the End of the Course

You will do the following skills tests during the testing lessons in the course:

- 1- and 2-Rescuer Adult BLS With AED
- 1- and 2-Rescuer Infant BLS

You will also do the written testing at the end of the course.

Steps for Testing CPR Skills

Follow these steps as you give the test to the students:

Step	Action
1	Write the student's name on the Skills Testing Sheet.
2	Test 2 students at a time. Test each student in each role. • Other students will continue practicing. • Students waiting for testing should not watch the test. • Do not give hints during the test.
3	Check the Skills Testing Sheet, 1 item at a time, as the student performs the BLS sequence. Check only those items on the checklist that the student performs correctly, according to the specific skills descriptions.
4	If the student did not perform a specific skill step or series of skills steps correctly, circle those areas on the Skills Testing Sheet. • Tell the student to focus on practicing those specific skill steps. • Retest the student during the Remediation lesson at the end of the course.
5	If the student is successful in correctly showing all steps on the skills testing checklist, mark the student as "passing" the test.
6	Test the next student, and so on, until you have tested all students once.
7	Tell students who need remediation to practice before retesting later in the course.
8	Retest any student who does not pass *as part of the Remediation lesson at the end of the course.*

Retesting Students

In every retesting case, test the student on the entire skill. In some instances you may defer retesting to a later time after the course. For example, if remediation is not successful, you might develop a plan of improvement and schedule retesting once the student completes that plan.

In situations where a student needs substantial additional remediation, you may recommend that the student repeat the BLS for Healthcare Providers Course.

Using a Stopwatch

The skills tests that measure the rate of compressions require that you use a stopwatch. Follow these rules when using a stopwatch:

- Start your stopwatch when the student first compresses the sternum.
- Stop your stopwatch at the end of the 30th compression for adult or 1-rescuer infant CPR or at the end of the 15th compression for 2-rescuer infant CPR.
- Mark the step "correct" if the number of seconds is 18 or less for adult or 1-rescuer infant CPR or 9 seconds or less for 2-rescuer infant CPR.

Starting the 1- and 2-Rescuer Adult or Infant BLS Skills Test

Before the 1- and 2-Rescuer Adult or Infant BLS Skills Test, read the following testing script aloud to the student (may be read to all students at once):

This test is like a realistic emergency situation: you should do whatever you think is necessary to save the victim's life. You will have to determine for yourself what you need to do. For example, if you check the response on the manikin and there is no response, then you should do whatever you would do for a person who is not responding.

I won't tell you about the condition of the victim once you start, and I won't be able to answer any questions. You can treat me like a bystander and tell me to do something that you would tell a bystander to do. If you make a mistake or forget to do something important, you should not stop. Just do your best to correct the error. Please continue doing what you would do in an actual emergency until I tell you to stop.

Do you have any questions before we start?

After starting, if the student asks any questions about BLS skills or sequences, you should not answer him or her. Rather, tell the student, "Do what you think is best right now."

If the student asks questions about what to do with the manikin, tell him or her, "Check the manikin yourself and do what you think is needed to save a life."

If the student seems unsure, do your best to explain that he or she will be assessing the manikin and doing whatever is necessary.

Then read this specific situation to begin the 1-Rescuer **Adult** BLS Skills Test (2-Rescuer Adult BLS Skills Test to follow):

This is a test of the 1- and 2-rescuer adult BLS skills. The scene is safe for you to enter and you are wearing protective gloves. A woman collapsed a few minutes earlier in front of witnesses, and there is no risk of a head or spinal cord injury. You are the only healthcare provider on the scene. You can treat me like a bystander and tell me to do something that you would tell a bystander to do. The emergency plan at the site is to call 911. You have a pocket mask and you do not know if an AED is available.

Start now by doing what you would do in an actual emergency, and don't stop until I tell you to.

Read this specific situation to begin the 1-Rescuer **Infant** BLS Skills Test (2-Rescuer Infant BLS Skills Test to follow):

This is a test of the 1- and 2-rescuer infant BLS skills. The scene is safe for you to enter and you are wearing protective gloves. A mother comes to you with her 6-month-old infant, who is not breathing. There is no risk of a head or spinal cord injury. You are the only healthcare provider on the scene. You can treat me like a bystander and tell me to do something that you would tell a bystander to do. The emergency plan at the site is to call 911. You have a pocket mask and you do not know if an AED is available.

Start now by doing what you would do in an actual emergency, and don't stop until I tell you to.

Remediation

Remediation Lesson

At times you will have to provide remediation to a student who is having trouble with portions of the course. If a student does not show mastery of psychomotor skills or does not score at least 84% on the written test, determine where the student is having trouble.

You may need to do one or more of the following:

- Replay sections of the video or practice skills to ensure learning.
- Help the students with additional practice.

Once you work with the students:

- Have the students retake the written test if necessary.
- Retest skills as necessary.

After the Course

Program Evaluation

The AHA strives to continually improve our training materials. One way to ensure constructive feedback is to gather program evaluation forms from each student.

After the students complete the written test, ask them to complete a program evaluation. Retain course evaluations as directed in the *Program Administration Manual.*

You should review the evaluation forms after each class. Note the good things that students indicate, and strive to improve your performance in future courses based on other comments.

Issuing Cards

Once the instructor submits the roster to the Training Center for processing, the Training Center will issue completion cards to each student who

- Demonstrates competency in each of the specified skills by passing the required skills tests
- Scores at least 84% on the written test

Additional Resources

Self-Directed Learning Courses

BLS for Healthcare Providers Online Courses

The AHA has options for computer-based ECC courses: BLS for Healthcare Providers Online and HeartCode BLS. These courses are available at **OnlineAHA.org.**

All credentialed AHA online courses have the following parts:

Part	Details
Part 1: Online Cognitive Course and Written Test	Upon successful completion of Part 1, students should print the completion certificate and present it to the BLS Instructor.
Parts 2 and 3: Practice Session and Skills Test	Part 2 allows the student to practice the physical skills the student learned online, to ask questions, and to receive coaching from the BLS Instructor. For Part 3, the instructor will TEST the student. Do not prompt the students as referenced above. The test should be conducted by using the same Skills Testing Sheets found in the *BLS for Healthcare Providers Instructor Manual.*

Additional AHA Courses

Courses That a BLS Instructor Can Teach

Certified BLS Instructors can teach several AHA courses:

- BLS for Healthcare Providers Course
- Heartsaver courses
- Community courses

Advanced Cardiovascular Life Support/ Pediatric Advanced Life Support Courses

The AHA has designed its advanced life support courses (ACLS and PALS) with basic life support skills as the foundation. As a BLS Instructor, you may be asked to test students in an advanced course who need a BLS Healthcare Provider card. You can test the student in BLS by using the BLS for Healthcare Providers Skills Testing Sheets. The student must also take the BLS Healthcare Provider written test and score at least 84%. A student who attempts this method to obtain a BLS Healthcare Provider course completion card is not permitted any remediation.

Recruiting and Mentoring New Instructors

Recruiting and Mentoring Instructors

As a current AHA Instructor, you may have students in your course who want to become an AHA BLS Instructor. The AHA encourages you to take a moment to pass along the information below to all students who are interested in becoming an instructor, after they successfully complete the provider course.

An AHA instructor course teaches the methods needed to effectively instruct others in resuscitation courses. The AHA requires that instructors be at least 16 years of age for Heartsaver Instructor and BLS Instructor courses.

Instructor Candidate Selection

The ideal instructor candidate

- Is motivated to teach
- Is motivated to facilitate learning
- Is motivated to ensure that students acquire the skills necessary for successful course completion
- Views student assessment as a way to improve individual knowledge and skills

Instructor Course Prerequisites

Prospective participants in an AHA instructor course must

- Have current provider status in the discipline they wish to teach
- Have completed an Instructor Candidate Application (obtained from the Training Center Coordinator)
- Complete the AHA Core Instructor Course

Science Update Information

Update on 2010 AHA Guidelines for CPR and ECC

For detailed information on the science changes in the *2010 AHA Guidelines for CPR and ECC,* see *Highlights of the 2010 AHA Guidelines for CPR and ECC,* available at **www.heart.org/eccguidelines**.

Part 5

BLS for Healthcare Providers Lesson Maps

HCP
PRE
A

30 Days Before Course

Your Role

- Determine course specifics
  - Target audience
  - Number of students
  - Special needs or equipment
- Reserve equipment
- Schedule room
- Schedule additional instructors if needed

Reference

HCP Instructor Manual

© 2011 American Heart Association

HCP
PRE
B

2 Weeks Before Course

Your Role
- Send student precourse letters with student materials
- Confirm additional instructors

Reference
HCP Instructor Manual

© 2011 American Heart Association

HCP
PRE
C

Day Before Course

Your Role
- Set up room
- Coordinate plan with additional instructors if needed
- Use precourse checklist to ensure that all equipment is available and working
- Ensure that all course paperwork is in order

Sample Floor Plan

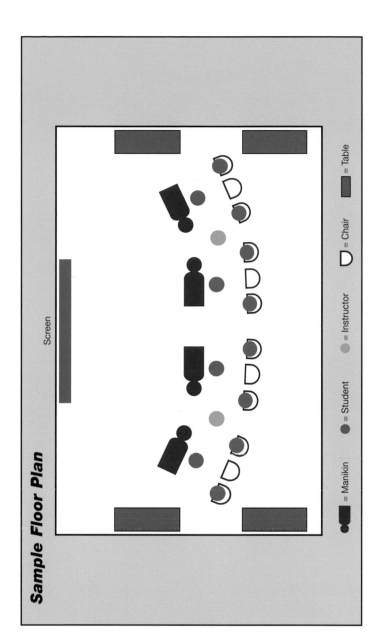

Screen

■ = Manikin ● = Student ● = Instructor D = Chair ■ = Table

Reference
HCP Instructor Manual

© 2011 American Heart Association

Day of Course

Your Role
- Make sure all equipment is working
- Have DVD ready to play before students arrive
- Pass out supplies
- Greet students as they arrive to help make them feel at ease
- Fill out course roster

Reference
HCP Instructor Manual

© 2011 American Heart Association

HCP 1

Course Introduction

0:00 → 5:00

Your Role

- Introduce instructors
- Invite students to introduce themselves in small groups
- Explain housekeeping issues, including paperwork and facilities
- Explain that the course is somewhat strenuous
- Ask that anyone with a medical concern, such as knee or back problems, talk with one of the instructors
- Explain how students will learn by video-based, practice-while-watching, and practice sessions
- Tell the students, "We are scheduled to end at _____."

Reference

None

Resources

- Course roster

Student Role

- Introduce self
- Listen to instructor

Student Objectives

- Get acquainted with instructors and other students

HCP
2

Course Overview and 2010 AHA Guidelines for CPR and ECC Science Update

0:00 → 12:00

Your Role
- Show video
- Tell students to follow along in HCP Student Manual

Reference
HCP Student Manual, *2010 AHA Guidelines for CPR and ECC Science Update*

Resources
- AV equipment

Student Role
- Watch video
- Follow along in manual

Student Objectives
- See demonstration of CPR
- Understand science updates from *2010 AHA Guidelines for CPR and ECC*

© 2011 American Heart Association

HCP
3

BLS/CPR Basics for Adults

0:00 → 1:00

Your Role

- Show video
- Tell students to follow along in HCP Student Manual

Reference

HCP Student Manual, *BLS/CPR for Adults*

Resources

- AV equipment

Student Role

- Watch video
- Follow along in manual

Student Objectives

- See full sequence of CPR
- Get motivated to learn CPR

© 2011 American Heart Association

HCP
4

1-Rescuer CPR With AED Demo

0:00 → 1:00

Your Role

- Video continues
- Do NOT redemonstrate skills

Reference

HCP Student Manual, *Understanding the Basics of BLS*

Resources

- AV equipment

Student Role

- Watch video

Student Objectives

- Understand full sequence of 1-rescuer CPR with pocket mask and AED

© 2011 American Heart Association

HCP
5

Assessment and Scene Safety

0:00 → 1:00

Your Role

- Video continues
- Mention any personal protective equipment requirements for students' work environment, if known

Reference

HCP Student Manual, Step 1: *Assessment and Scene Safety,* Step 2: *Activate the Emergency Response System and Get an AED,* and Step 3: *Pulse Check*

Resources

- AV equipment

Student Role

- Watch video

Student Objectives

- Understand how to check for scene safety
- Understand how to assess responsiveness
- Understand importance of activating the emergency response system and getting the AED
- Understand importance of doing a pulse check in 5 to 10 seconds

© 2011 American Heart Association

PWW

HCP
6

Chest Compressions for Adult Victims
(Video Intro, Then Practice)

0:00 → 8:00

Your Role
- Assign students to groups
- Ask first student in each group to get into position
- Show video
- Do NOT redemonstrate skills
- Students practice with video; rotate among all students
- Carefully observe each student
- Give positive and corrective feedback
- Emphasize core concepts: push hard, push fast; allow complete chest recoil; when giving breaths watch for chest rise; minimize interruptions

Reference
HCP Student Manual, *Chest Compression Technique*

Resources
- AV equipment
- Adult manikin
- Stopwatches

Student Role
- Practice while watching video

Student Objectives
- Perform chest compressions
- Show proper hand position
- Perform 5 sets of 30 compressions to correct depth without stopping
- Push hard, push fast
- Allow complete chest recoil

© 2011 American Heart Association

HCP
7
Airway and Breathing

0:00 → 6:00

Resources
- AV equipment
- Adult manikins
- Pocket masks
- One-way valves

Student Role
- Practice while watching video

Student Objectives
- Perform head tilt–chin lift
- Give 5 sets of 2 breaths with mask

Your Role
- Show video
- Do NOT redemonstrate skills
- Students practice with video; rotate among all students
- Carefully observe each student
- Give corrective feedback
- Emphasize visible chest rise

Reference
HCP Student Manual, *Opening the Airway for Breaths: Head Tilt–Chin Lift and Giving Adult Mouth-to-Mask Breaths*

© 2011 American Heart Association

HCP
8

Adult Compressions and Breaths *Practice*

0:00 → 8:00

PWW

Your Role

- Video continues
- Do NOT redemonstrate skills
- Students practice with video; rotate among all students
- Carefully observe each student
- Give corrective feedback
- Emphasize core concepts: push hard, push fast; allow complete chest recoil; when giving breaths watch for chest rise; minimize interruptions

Resources

- AV equipment
- Adult manikins
- Pocket masks
- One-way valves
- Stopwatches

Student Role

- Practice while watching video

Student Objectives

- Learn how to put compressions and breaths together with 30:2 ratio
- Perform 5 cycles of 30:2

Reference

HCP Student Manual, Step 4: *Begin Cycles of 30 Chest Compressions and 2 Breaths (CPR)*

© 2011 American Heart Association

9A

0:00

→

12:00

1-Rescuer Adult BLS
Practice Session
(Video Intro, Then Practice)

Your Role

- Video continues
- Have students rotate so each has a chance to practice
- Give corrective feedback

Reference

HCP Student Manual, *1- and 2-Rescuer Adult BLS With AED Skills Testing Sheet*

Resources

- AV equipment
- Adult manikins
- Pocket masks
- One-way valves
- Stopwatches

Student Role

- Watch video
- Demonstrate full sequence of CPR

Student Objectives

- Demonstrate full sequence of 1-rescuer CPR for adult

© 2011 American Heart Association

HCP
9B

1-Rescuer Adult BLS
Practice Session Details

Play video:

- S1 watches situation on video and responds as rescuer
- S1 practices entire sequence of 1-rescuer CPR for an adult

Rotate through other students responding to the situation on the video with entire sequence of 1-rescuer CPR for an adult

Carefully observe each student

Give positive and corrective feedback

© 2011 American Heart Association

Breaths With Bag-Mask for *Adult Victims*

0:00 → 12:00

PWW

Resources
- AV equipment
- Adult manikins
- Bag-masks

Student Role
- Practice while watching video

Student Objectives
- Perform head tilt–chin lift
- Give 5 sets of 2 breaths with bag-mask

Your Role
- Show video
- Do NOT redemonstrate skills
- Students practice with video; rotate among all students
- Carefully observe each student
- Give corrective feedback
- Emphasize visible chest rise

Reference
HCP Student Manual, *2 Rescuers Using the Bag-Mask*

© 2011 American Heart Association

HCP 11

2-Rescuer Adult BLS/ Team CPR Sequence

0:00 → 3:00

Your Role
- Video continues
- Do NOT redemonstrate skills

Reference
HCP Student Manual, 2-Rescuer Adult BLS/Team CPR Sequence

Resources
- AV equipment

Student Role
- Watch video

Student Objectives
- Understand how to do 2-rescuer CPR with an AED

© 2011 American Heart Association

0:00 → 3:00

Defibrillation:
AED Introduction and Use

Resources
- AV equipment

Student Role
- Watch video

Your Role
- Show video

Student Objectives
- Understand purpose of an AED

Reference
HCP Student Manual, *Automated External Defibrillator for Adults and Children 8 Years of Age and Older*

© 2011 American Heart Association

0:00 → 2:00

AED Special Situations and Safety

Your Role
- Show video

Reference
HCP Student Manual, *Special Situations*

Resources
- AV equipment

Student Role
- Watch video

Student Objectives
- Understand special situations when using an AED

© 2011 American Heart Association

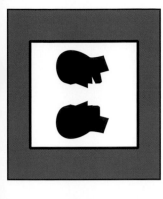

0:00 → 4:00

Using the AED Trainer

Your Role
- Explain how to use trainer
- Emphasize following AED prompts
- Tell students that AED trainer will not give a real shock

Reference
None

Resources
- AV equipment
- AED trainer
- AED supplies

Student Role
- Listen to instructor

Student Objectives
- Know how to use trainer

© 2011 American Heart Association

HCP
15A

1- and 2-Rescuer Adult BLS
With AED
Practice Session

0:00 →

25:00

Your Role

- Video continues
- Pause video
- Tell students to turn to practice sheet in HCP Student Manual
- Rotate among all students, each practicing being one of 2 rescuers performing all steps of CPR and using the AED
- Tell each student to instruct someone to activate the emergency response system and get the AED
- Carefully observe each student using the AED
- Give corrective feedback
- Emphasize following AED prompts

Reference

HCP Student Manual, *1- and 2-Rescuer Adult BLS With AED Skills Testing Sheet*

Resources

- AV equipment
- Adult manikins
- AED trainers
- AED supplies
- Pocket masks
- Bag-masks
- One-way valves
- Stopwatches

Student Role

- Watch video
- Demonstrate full sequence of CPR with AED

Student Objectives

- Show how to use an AED with all steps of 2-rescuer CPR

© 2011 American Heart Association

1- and 2-Rescuer Adult BLS
With AED
Practice Session Details

Rotations

<u>3:1 Student-to-Manikin Ratio</u>

1st Rotation: S2 starts CPR, S1 brings and uses AED, both do CPR; S3 observes

2nd Rotation: S3 starts CPR, S2 brings and uses AED, both do CPR; S1 observes

3rd Rotation: S1 starts CPR, S3 brings and uses AED, both do CPR; S2 observes

<u>2:1 Student-to-Manikin Ratio</u>

1st Rotation: S2 starts CPR, S1 brings and uses AED, both do CPR

2nd Rotation: S1 starts CPR, S2 brings and uses AED, both do CPR

<u>1:1 Student-to-Manikin Ratio</u>

Rotation: Two students combine as per 2:1

© 2011 American Heart Association

Introduction to Child BLS/CPR

0:00 → 2:00

Your Role
- Video continues

Reference
HCP Student Manual, *BLS/CPR Basics for Children From 1 Year of Age to Puberty*

Resources
- AV equipment

Student Role
- Watch video

Student Objectives
- Watch differences in CPR for child
- Recognize similarities and differences between adult and child CPR

© 2011 American Heart Association

PWW

Chest Compressions for Child Victims
(Video Intro, Then Practice)

0:00 → 5:00

Your Role

- Video continues
- Do NOT redemonstrate skills
- Students practice with video; rotate among all students
- Carefully observe each student
- Give positive and corrective feedback
- Emphasize core concepts: push hard, push fast; allow complete chest recoil; when giving breaths watch for chest rise; minimize interruptions

Reference

HCP Student Manual, *1-Handed Chest Compressions*

Resources

- AV equipment
- Adult or child manikins
- Stopwatches

Student Role

- Practice while watching video

Student Objectives

- Perform 1-handed chest compressions
- Show proper hand position
- Perform 5 sets of 30 compressions to correct depth without stopping
- Push hard, push fast
- Allow complete chest recoil

© 2011 American Heart Association

0:00 → 1:00

Introduction to Infant BLS/CPR

Your Role
- Video continues
- Tell students to follow along in HCP Student Manual

Reference
HCP Student Manual, *BLS/CPR Basics for Infants*

Resources
- AV equipment

Student Role
- Watch video
- Follow along in manual

Student Objectives
- See full sequence of CPR

© 2011 American Heart Association

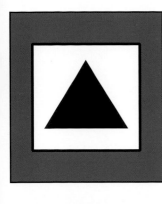

HCP
19

1- and 2-Rescuer Infant BLS/CPR Demo

0:00 → 2:00

Your Role
- Video continues

Reference
HCP Student Manual, *1-Rescuer Infant CPR and 2-Rescuer Infant CPR*

Resources
- AV equipment

Student Role
- Watch video

Student Objectives
- Understand full sequence of 1- and 2-rescuer CPR with mask

© 2011 American Heart Association

2-Finger Chest Compressions
for Infant Victims

0:00
→
7:00

PWW

Resources
- AV equipment
- Infant manikins

Student Role
- Practice while watching video

Student Objectives
- Perform chest compressions
- Show proper finger position (2-finger)
- Perform 5 sets of 30 compressions to correct depth without stopping
- Push hard, push fast
- Allow complete chest recoil

Your Role
- Video continues
- Do NOT redemonstrate skills
- Students practice with video; rotate among all students
- Carefully observe each student
- Give positive and corrective feedback
- Emphasize core concepts: push hard, push fast; allow complete chest recoil; when giving breaths watch for chest rise; minimize interruptions

Reference
HCP Student Manual, *2-Finger Chest Compression Technique*

© 2011 American Heart Association

HCP 21

Breaths With Bag-Mask for Infant Victims

0:00 → 4:00

PWW

Your Role
- Show video
- Do NOT redemonstrate skills
- Students practice with video; rotate among all students
- Carefully observe each student
- Give corrective feedback
- Emphasize visible chest rise

Reference
HCP Student Manual, *Infant Ventilation With Barrier Devices*

Resources
- AV equipment
- Infant manikins
- Bag-masks

Student Role
- Practice while watching video

Student Objectives
- Give 5 sets of 2 breaths with bag-mask
- Show chest rise with breaths

© 2011 American Heart Association

HCP
22

2-Rescuer Infant CPR/
2 Thumb–Encircling Hands
Chest Compressions for
Infant Victims

0:00

→

8:00

Your Role

- Video continues
- Do NOT redemonstrate skills
- Students practice with video; rotate among all students
- Carefully observe each student
- Give positive and corrective feedback
- Emphasize core concepts: push hard, push fast; allow complete chest recoil; when giving breaths watch for chest rise; minimize interruptions

Reference

HCP Student Manual, 2 Thumb–Encircling Hands Chest Compression Technique

Resources

- AV equipment
- Infant manikins

Student Role

- Practice while watching video

Student Objectives

- Perform chest compressions
- Show proper finger position (2 thumb–encircling hands)
- Perform 10 sets of 15 compressions to correct depth without stopping
- Push hard, push fast
- Allow complete chest recoil

© 2011 American Heart Association

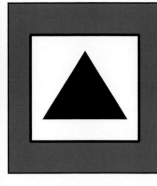

HCP
23A

1- and 2-Rescuer Infant BLS/CPR
Practice Session
(Video Intro, Then Practice)

0:00 → 11:00

Your Role

- Video continues
- Pause video
- Rotate among all students, each practicing being one of 2 rescuers performing all steps of CPR
- Tell each student to instruct someone to activate the emergency response system
- Give corrective feedback

Resources

- AV equipment
- Infant manikins
- Pocket masks
- Bag-masks
- One-way valves
- Stopwatches

Student Role

- Watch video
- Demonstrate full sequence of CPR

Student Objectives

- Show how to perform 2-rescuer CPR

Reference

HCP Student Manual, *1- and 2-Rescuer Infant BLS Skills Testing Sheet*

© 2011 American Heart Association

Rotations

3:1 Student-to-Manikin Ratio

1st Rotation: S1 assesses and starts breathing; S2 compresses; S3 observes

2nd Rotation: S2 assesses and starts breathing; S3 compresses; S1 observes

3rd Rotation: S3 assesses and starts breathing; S1 compresses; S2 observes

2:1 Student-to-Manikin Ratio

1st Rotation: S1 assesses and starts breathing; S2 compresses

2nd Rotation: S2 assesses and starts breathing; S1 compresses

1:1 Student-to-Manikin Ratio

Rotation: Two students combine as per 2:1

© 2011 American Heart Association

0:00 → 2:00

AED for Infants and for Children *From 1 to 8 Years of Age*

Your Role
- Show video

Reference
HCP Student Manual, *Automated External Defibrillator for Infants and for Children From 1 to 8 Years of Age*

Resources
- AV equipment

Student Role
- Watch video

Student Objectives
- Understand how to use an AED on an infant or child from 1 to 8 years of age

© 2011 American Heart Association

HCP
25

CPR With an Advanced Airway

0:00 → 1:00

Your Role
- Video continues

Resources
- AV equipment

Student Role
- Watch video

Student Objectives
- Know how to do 2-rescuer CPR with an advanced airway in place

Reference
HCP Student Manual, CPR With an Advanced Airway

© 2011 American Heart Association

Rescue Breathing

0:00 → 4:00

Your Role
- Video continues

Resources
- AV equipment

Student Role
- Watch video

Student Objectives
- Know how to do rescue breathing for adults, children, and infants

Reference
HCP Student Manual, *Rescue Breathing*

© 2011 American Heart Association

HCP
27

Mouth-to-Mouth Breaths for Victims 1 Year of Age and Older

0:00 →

1:00

Resources
- AV equipment

Student Role
- Watch video

Student Objectives
- Know how to give mouth-to-mouth breaths for victims 1 year of age and older

Your Role
- Video continues

Reference

HCP Student Manual, *Mouth-to-Mouth Breaths*

© 2011 American Heart Association

0:00

→

2:00

Adult/Child Choking (Responsive) (Video Intro)

Resources
- AV equipment

Student Role
- Watch video

Student Objectives
- Understand how to relieve choking in victims 1 year of age and older

Your Role
- Video continues

Reference
HCP Student Manual, *Relief of Choking in Victims 1 Year of Age and Older*

© 2011 American Heart Association

OPTIONAL

HCP
28B

Adult/Child Choking (Responsive) Optional Practice

Your Role
- Video continues
- All students can rotate through optional practice
- If optional practice is conducted, guide student through hand placement
- Instructor will need to manually pause video for optional practice

Resources
- AV equipment
- Adult manikins

Student Role
- Optional practice

Student Objectives
- Show how to relieve choking in victims 1 year of age and older

Reference
HCP Student Manual, *Relief of Choking in Victims 1 Year of Age and Older*

© 2011 American Heart Association

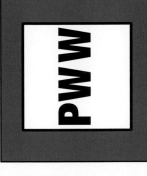

PWW

HCP
28C

Adult/Child Choking (Responsive)
Optional Practice Session Details

Students can practice correct hand placement for abdominal thrusts on adult manikin during optional practice

Assessment question is "Are you choking?"

Carefully observe each student

Give corrective feedback

Watch for correct hand placement

© 2011 American Heart Association

Adult/Child Choking (Unresponsive)

Resources
- AV equipment

Student Role
- Watch video

Student Objectives
- Know to activate the emergency response system once a choking victim becomes unresponsive
- Know to start CPR if a choking adult or child becomes unresponsive

Your Role
- Video continues
- This is only a video demonstration, with no student practice

Reference
HCP Student Manual, *Relief of Choking in Victims 1 Year of Age and Older*

© 2011 American Heart Association

HCP
30A

0:00 → 6:00

*Infant Choking
(Responsive)*

Resources
- AV equipment
- Infant manikins

Student Role
- Practice while watching video

Student Objectives
- Identify the signs of choking in a responsive infant
- Show how to relieve choking in a responsive infant

Your Role
- Show video
- Students practice relieving choking by using back slaps and chest thrusts
- All students rotate through practice

Reference
HCP Student Manual, *Relief of Choking in Infants*

© 2011 American Heart Association

PWW

30B

Infant Choking (Responsive)
Practice Session Details

Students practice correct technique for back slaps and chest thrusts on infant manikin

Carefully observe each student

Give corrective feedback

Make sure students use correct technique

© 2011 American Heart Association

0:00 → 1:00

Infant Choking (Unresponsive)

Your Role
- Video continues

Reference
HCP Student Manual, *Relief of Choking in Infants*

Resources
- AV equipment

Student Role
- Watch video

Student Objectives
- Know to activate the emergency response system once a choking infant becomes unresponsive
- Know to start CPR if a choking infant becomes unresponsive

© 2011 American Heart Association

HCP
32
Course Summary and Closure

0:00 → 1:00

Your Role
- Video continues
- Stop video

Reference
None

Resources
- AV equipment

Student Role
- Watch video

Student Objectives
- None

© 2011 American Heart Association

HCP
33A

33 34/35

Written Test

0:00 → 25:00

Your Role
- Divide students into 2 groups: half do written test (Lesson 33) and half do skills test (Lessons 34 and 35); then groups switch
- Distribute answer sheets
- Pass out tests
- Tell students to answer questions
- Ask students not to write on tests
- Collect tests
- Grade tests
- Pass out course evaluation forms
- Tell students to complete evaluation forms
- Collect completed evaluation forms

Resources
- Tests
- Pencils
- Answer sheets
- Course evaluation forms (print from Instructor Network)

Student Role
- Take test
- Complete course evaluation form

Student Objectives
- Show mastery of cognitive information

© 2011 American Heart Association

Written Test Details

The written test is a closed-book test

Students may not cooperate or talk to each other during the test

When student completes the test, grade the test

Answer any questions

Students who scored <84% need immediate remediation:

- Make sure students understand errors and correct answers

- Provide remediation by giving second test or by having students verbally go over each item they got incorrect, showing understanding of incorrect items

© 2011 American Heart Association

HCP
34A

0:00 → 30:00

1- and 2-Rescuer
Adult BLS With AED
Skills Test

T

Your Role

- Rotate among all students, each practicing being one of 2 rescuers performing all steps of CPR and using the AED
- Tell each student to instruct someone to activate the emergency response system and get the AED
- Carefully observe each student using the AED
- SKILLS TEST: Evaluate students' competency in 2-rescuer CPR with bag-mask
- Check off each skill as student demonstrates competency
- Emphasize following AED prompts

Reference

HCP Instructor Manual, *1- and 2-Rescuer Adult BLS With AED Skills Testing Sheet Criteria*

Resources

- AV equipment
- Adult manikins
- AED trainers
- AED supplies
- Pocket masks
- Bag-masks
- One-way valves
- Stopwatches

Student Role

- Watch video
- Demonstrate full sequence of CPR with AED

Student Objectives

- Show how to use an AED with all steps of 2-rescuer CPR
- Show competency in each skill of 2-rescuer CPR and AED

1- and 2-Rescuer
Adult BLS With AED
Skills Test Details

Rotations

<u>3:1 Student-to-Manikin Ratio</u>

1st Rotation: S2 starts CPR, S1 brings and uses AED, both do CPR; S1 is tested on AED and team compressions, S2 is tested on 1-rescuer CPR and bag-mask

2nd Rotation: S3 starts CPR, S2 brings and uses AED, both do CPR; S2 is tested on AED and team compressions, S3 is tested on 1-rescuer CPR and bag-mask

3rd Rotation: S1 starts CPR, S3 brings and uses AED, both do CPR; S3 is tested on AED and team compressions, S1 is tested on 1-rescuer CPR and bag-mask

<u>2:1 Student-to-Manikin Ratio</u>

1st Rotation: S2 starts CPR, S1 brings and uses AED, both do CPR; S1 is tested on AED and team compressions, S2 is tested on 1-rescuer CPR and bag-mask

2nd Rotation: S1 starts CPR, S2 brings and uses AED, both do CPR; S2 is tested on AED and team compressions, S1 is tested on 1-rescuer CPR and bag-mask

<u>1:1 Student-to-Manikin Ratio</u>

Rotation: Two students combine as per 2:1

© 2011 American Heart Association

1- and 2-Rescuer
Infant BLS
Skills Test

0:00
→
30:00

Resources
- AV equipment
- Infant manikins
- Pocket masks
- Bag-masks
- One-way valves
- Stopwatches

Student Role
- Demonstrate full sequence of CPR

Student Objectives
- Show how to perform 1- and 2-rescuer CPR
- Take test on each skill

Your Role
- Rotate among all students, each practicing being one of 2 rescuers performing all steps of CPR
- Tell each student to tell someone to activate the emergency response system
- SKILLS TEST: Evaluate students' competency in 1- and 2-rescuer CPR with bag-mask
- Check off each skill as student demonstrates competency
- Refer student for remediation if unsuccessful on test

Reference
HCP Instructor Manual, *1- and 2-Rescuer Infant BLS Skills Testing Sheet Criteria*

© 2011 American Heart Association

1- and 2-Rescuer
Infant BLS
Skills Test Details

Rotations

Student starts CPR and does 2 cycles; student is tested in 1-rescuer CPR (with pocket mask for breathing)

Another student comes in as 2nd rescuer, takes over breathing with bag-mask

First student continues 2-rescuer CPR as compressor for 2 cycles, then switches, takes over bag-mask breathing for 2 cycles; student is tested in 2-rescuer CPR

3:1 Student-to-Manikin Ratio

1st Rotation: S1 starts CPR, S2 is 2nd rescuer; S1 is tested

2nd Rotation: S2 starts CPR, S3 is 2nd rescuer; S2 is tested

3rd Rotation: S3 starts CPR, S1 is 2nd rescuer; S3 is tested

2:1 Student-to-Manikin Ratio

1st Rotation: S1 starts CPR, S2 is 2nd rescuer; S1 is tested

2nd Rotation: S2 starts CPR, S1 is 2nd rescuer; S2 is tested

1:1 Student-to-Manikin Ratio

Rotation: Two students combine as per 2:1

© 2011 American Heart Association

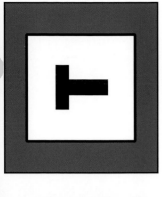

HCP
36

Remediation

0:00 → **Variable**

Your Role

- Determine where student is having trouble
- Replay sections of video or practice skills to ensure learning
- Redo written test if student scored <84%
- Retest skills as necessary
- Some students may need additional practice or may need to repeat the course to demonstrate skills competency and to achieve a course completion card

Resources

- HCP Student Manual
- Test version B
- Manikins
- AED trainers
- AED supplies
- Pocket masks
- Bag-masks
- One-way valves

Student Role

- Learn skills not previously learned
- Practice skills

Student Objectives

- Show competency in skills required for successful course completion

© 2011 American Heart Association

Immediately After Course

Your Role

- Collect and arrange all course paperwork
- Rearrange room
- Clean and store equipment
- Fill out Training Center course report forms
- Read and consider comments from course evaluations
- Send students course completion cards if not already distributed

Reference

HCP Instructor Manual

© 2011 American Heart Association

Part 6

BLS for Healthcare Providers Renewal Lesson Maps

HCP-R
PRE
A

30 Days Before Course

Your Role

- Determine course specifics
  - Target audience
  - Number of students
  - Special needs or equipment
- Reserve equipment
- Schedule room
- Schedule additional instructors if needed

Reference

HCP Instructor Manual

© 2011 American Heart Association

HCP-R
PRE
B

2 Weeks Before Course

Your Role
- Send student precourse letters with student materials
- Confirm additional instructors

Reference
HCP Instructor Manual

© 2011 American Heart Association

Day Before Course

Sample Floor Plan

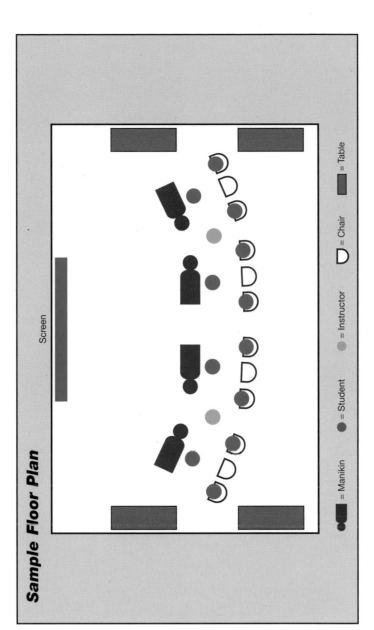

Screen

= Manikin   ● = Student   ● = Instructor   D = Chair   ▬ = Table

Your Role

- Set up room
- Coordinate plan with additional instructors if needed
- Use precourse checklist to ensure that all equipment is available and working
- Ensure that all course paperwork is in order

Reference

HCP Instructor Manual

© 2011 American Heart Association

Day of Course

Your Role

- Make sure all equipment is working
- Have DVD ready to play before students arrive
- Pass out supplies
- Greet students as they arrive to help make them feel at ease
- Fill out course roster

Reference

HCP Instructor Manual

© 2011 American Heart Association

Course Introduction

0:00 → 5:00

Your Role

- Introduce instructors
- Invite students to introduce themselves in small groups
- Explain housekeeping issues, including paperwork and facilities
- Explain that the course is somewhat strenuous
- Ask that anyone with a medical concern, such as knee or back problems, talk with one of the instructors
- Explain how students will learn by video-based, practice-while-watching, and practice sessions
- Tell the students, "We are scheduled to end at _____."

Reference

None

Resources

- Course roster

Student Role

- Introduce self
- Listen to instructor

Student Objectives

- Get acquainted with instructors and other students

© 2011 American Heart Association

HCP-R
2

Course Overview and 2010 AHA Guidelines for CPR and ECC Science Update

0:00 → 12:00

Your Role
- Show video
- Tell students to follow along in HCP Student Manual

Reference
HCP Student Manual, *2010 AHA Guidelines for CPR and ECC Science Update*

Resources
- AV equipment

Student Role
- Watch video
- Follow along in manual

Student Objectives
- See demonstration of CPR
- Understand science updates from *2010 AHA Guidelines for CPR and ECC*

© 2011 American Heart Association

HCP-R
3

0:00 → 1:00

BLS/CPR Basics for Adults

Your Role
- Show video
- Tell students to follow along in HCP Student Manual

Reference
HCP Student Manual, *BLS/CPR for Adults*

Resources
- AV equipment

Student Role
- Watch video
- Follow along in manual

Student Objectives
- See full sequence of CPR
- Get motivated to learn CPR

© 2011 American Heart Association

HCP-R

4

2-Rescuer CPR With AED
Demo

0:00 → 1:00

Your Role
- Video continues
- Do NOT redemonstrate skills

Reference
HCP Student Manual, *2-Rescuer Adult BLS/Team CPR Sequence*

Resources
- AV equipment

Student Role
- Watch video

Student Objectives
- Understand full sequence of 2-rescuer CPR with AED

© 2011 American Heart Association

HCP-R
5

Assessment and Scene Safety

0:00 → 1:00

Resources
- AV equipment

Student Role
- Watch video

Student Objectives
- Understand how to check for scene safety
- Understand how to assess responsiveness
- Understand importance of activating the emergency response system and getting the AED
- Understand importance of doing a pulse check in 5 to 10 seconds

Your Role
- Video continues

Reference
HCP Student Manual, Step 1: *Assessment and Scene Safety,* Step 2: *Activate the Emergency Response System and Get an AED,* and Step 3: *Pulse Check*

PWW

HCP-R

6

Chest Compressions for *Adult Victims* *(Video Intro, Then Practice)*

0:00 → 8:00

Your Role
- Assign students to groups
- Ask first student in each group to get into position
- Show video
- Do NOT redemonstrate skills
- Students practice with video; rotate among all students
- Carefully observe each student
- Give positive and corrective feedback
- Emphasize core concepts: push hard, push fast; allow complete chest recoil; when giving breaths watch for chest rise; minimize interruptions

Reference
HCP Student Manual, *Chest Compression Technique*

Resources
- AV equipment
- Adult manikin
- Stopwatches

Student Role
- Practice while watching video

Student Objectives
- Perform chest compressions
- Show proper hand position
- Perform 5 sets of 30 compressions to correct depth without stopping
- Push hard, push fast
- Allow complete chest recoil

© 2011 American Heart Association

Airway and Breathing

0:00 → 6:00

PWW

Resources

- AV equipment
- Adult manikins
- Pocket masks
- One-way valves

Student Role

- Practice while watching video

Student Objectives

- Perform head tilt-chin lift
- Give 5 sets of 2 breaths with mask

Your Role

- Show video
- Do NOT redemonstrate skills
- Students practice with video; rotate among all students
- Carefully observe each student
- Give corrective feedback
- Emphasize visible chest rise

Reference

HCP Student Manual, *Opening the Airway for Breaths: Head Tilt–Chin Lift and Giving Adult Mouth-to-Mask Breaths*

© 2011 American Heart Association

PWW

HCP-R
8

Breaths With Bag-Mask for Adult Victims

0:00 → 8:00

Your Role
- Show video
- Do NOT redemonstrate skills
- Students practice with video; rotate among all students
- Carefully observe each student
- Give corrective feedback
- Emphasize visible chest rise

Reference
HCP Student Manual, *2 Rescuers Using the Bag-Mask*

Resources
- AV equipment
- Adult manikins
- Bag-masks

Student Role
- Practice while watching video

Student Objectives
- Perform head tilt–chin lift
- Give 5 sets of 2 breaths with bag-mask

© 2011 American Heart Association

PWW

9

Adult Compressions and Breaths Practice

0:00 → 8:00

Your Role

- Video continues
- Do NOT redemonstrate skills
- Students practice with video; rotate among all students
- Carefully observe each student
- Give corrective feedback
- Emphasize core concepts: push hard, push fast; allow complete chest recoil; when giving breaths watch for chest rise; minimize interruptions

Reference

HCP Student Manual, *Step 4: Begin Cycles of 30 Chest Compressions and 2 Breaths (CPR)*

Resources

- AV equipment
- Adult manikins
- Pocket masks
- One-way valves
- Stopwatches

Student Role

- Practice while watching video

Student Objectives

- Learn how to put compressions and breaths together with 30:2 ratio
- Perform 5 cycles of 30:2

© 2011 American Heart Association

2-Rescuer Adult BLS/Team CPR Sequence

0:00 → 3:00

Your Role

- Video continues
- Do NOT redemonstrate skills

Reference

HCP Student Manual, 2-Rescuer Adult BLS/Team CPR Sequence

Resources

- AV equipment

Student Role

- Watch video

Student Objectives

- Understand how to do 2-rescuer CPR with an AED

© 2011 American Heart Association

Defibrillation:
AED Introduction and Use

0:00 → 3:00

Your Role
- Show video

Resources
- AV equipment

Student Role
- Watch video

Student Objectives
- Understand purpose of an AED

Reference
HCP Student Manual, *Automated External Defibrillator for Adults and Children 8 Years of Age and Older*

© 2011 American Heart Association

HCP-R
12

Using the AED Trainer

0:00 → 4:00

Your Role

- Explain how to use trainer
- Emphasize following AED prompts
- Tell students that AED trainer will not give a real shock

Reference

None

Resources

- AV equipment
- AED trainers
- AED supplies

Student Role

- Listen to instructor

Student Objectives

- Know how to use trainer

© 2011 American Heart Association

13A

1- and 2-Rescuer Adult BLS
With AED
Practice Session

0:00
→
16:00

Your Role

- Video continues
- Pause video
- Tell students to turn to practice sheet in HCP Student Manual
- Rotate among all students, each practicing being one of 2 rescuers performing all steps of CPR and using the AED
- Tell each student to instruct someone to activate the emergency response system and get the AED
- Carefully observe each student using the AED
- Give corrective feedback
- Emphasize following AED prompts

Reference

HCP Student Manual, *1- and 2-Rescuer Adult BLS With AED Skills Testing Sheet*

Resources

- AV equipment
- Adult manikins
- AED trainers
- AED supplies
- Pocket masks
- Bag-masks
- One-way valves
- Stopwatches

Student Role

- Watch video
- Demonstrate full sequence of CPR with AED

Student Objectives

- Show how to use an AED with all steps of 2-rescuer CPR

© 2011 American Heart Association

1- and 2-Rescuer Adult BLS
With AED
Practice Session Details

Rotations

<u>3:1 Student-to-Manikin Ratio</u>

1st Rotation: S2 starts CPR, S1 brings and uses AED, both do CPR; S3 observes and provides feedback

2nd Rotation: S3 starts CPR, S2 brings and uses AED, both do CPR; S1 observes and provides feedback

3rd Rotation: S1 starts CPR, S3 brings and uses AED, both do CPR; S2 observes and provides feedback

<u>2:1 Student-to-Manikin Ratio</u>

1st Rotation: S2 starts CPR, S1 brings and uses AED, both do CPR

2nd Rotation: S1 starts CPR, S2 brings and uses AED, both do CPR

<u>1:1 Student-to-Manikin Ratio</u>

Rotation: Two students combine as per 2:1

© 2011 American Heart Association

HCP-R
14

Introduction to Child BLS/CPR

0:00
→
2:00

Your Role
- Video continues

Reference
HCP Student Manual, *BLS/CPR Basics for Children From 1 Year of Age to Puberty*

Resources
- AV equipment

Student Role
- Watch video

Student Objectives
- Watch differences in CPR for child
- Recognize similarities and differences between adult and child CPR

© 2011 American Heart Association

PWW

HCP-R 15

Chest Compressions for Child Victims
(Video Intro, Then Practice)

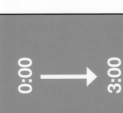

0:00 → 3:00

Your Role
- Video continues
- Do NOT redemonstrate skills
- Students practice with video; rotate among all students
- Carefully observe each student
- Give positive and corrective feedback
- Emphasize core concepts: push hard, push fast; allow complete chest recoil; when giving breaths watch for chest rise; minimize interruptions

Resources
- AV equipment
- Adult or child manikins
- Stopwatches

Student Role
- Practice while watching video

Student Objectives
- Perform 1-handed chest compressions
- Show proper hand position
- Perform 5 sets of 30 compres-sions to correct depth without stopping
- Push hard, push fast
- Allow complete chest recoil

Reference
HCP Student Manual, *1-Handed Chest Compressions*

© 2011 American Heart Association

HCP-R
16

Introduction to Infant BLS/CPR

0:00 → 3:00

Resources
- AV equipment

Student Role
- Watch video
- Follow along in manual

Student Objectives
- See full sequence of CPR

Your Role
- Video continues
- Tell students to follow along in HCP Student Manual

Reference
HCP Student Manual, *BLS/CPR Basics for Infants*

© 2011 American Heart Association

HCP-R
17

1- and 2-Rescuer Infant BLS/CPR Demo

0:00 → 3:00

Your Role
- Video continues

Resources
- AV equipment

Student Role
- Watch video

Student Objectives
- Understand full sequence of 1- and 2-rescuer CPR with mask

Reference
HCP Student Manual, *1-Rescuer Infant CPR and 2-Rescuer Infant CPR*

© 2011 American Heart Association

HCP-R
18A

1- and 2-Rescuer Infant BLS/CPR
Practice Session
(Video Intro, Then Practice)

0:00

→

10:00

Your Role
- Video continues
- Pause video
- Rotate among all students, each practicing being one of 2 rescuers performing all steps of CPR
- Tell each student to instruct someone to activate the emergency response system
- Give corrective feedback

Resources
- AV equipment
- Infant manikins
- Pocket masks
- Bag-masks
- One-way valves
- Stopwatches

Student Role
- Watch video
- Demonstrate full sequence of CPR

Student Objectives
- Show how to perform 2-rescuer CPR

Reference
HCP Student Manual, *1- and 2-Rescuer Infant BLS Skills Testing Sheet*

© 2011 American Heart Association

Rotations

3:1 Student-to-Manikin Ratio

1st Rotation: S1 assesses and starts breathing; S2 compresses; S3 observes and provides feedback

2nd Rotation: S2 assesses and starts breathing; S3 compresses; S1 observes and provides feedback

3rd Rotation: S3 assesses and starts breathing; S1 compresses; S2 observes and provides feedback

2:1 Student-to-Manikin Ratio

1st Rotation: S1 assesses and starts breathing; S2 compresses

2nd Rotation: S2 assesses and starts breathing; S1 compresses

1:1 Student-to-Manikin Ratio

Rotation: Two students combine as per 2:1

© 2011 American Heart Association

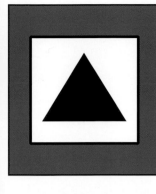

HCP-R
19

AED for Infants and for Children
From 1 to 8 Years of Age

0:00 → 1:00

Your Role
- Show video

Resources
- AV equipment

Student Role
- Watch video

Student Objectives
- Understand how to use an AED on an infant or child from 1 to 8 years of age

Reference
HCP Student Manual, *Automated External Defibrillator for Infants and for Children From 1 to 8 Years of Age*

© 2011 American Heart Association

HCP-R
20

CPR With an Advanced Airway

0:00 → 1:00

Resources
- AV equipment

Student Role
- Watch video

Student Objectives
- Know how to do 2-rescuer CPR with an advanced airway in place

Your Role
- Video continues

Reference
HCP Student Manual, *CPR With an Advanced Airway*

© 2011 American Heart Association

HCP-R
21

Rescue Breathing

0:00 → 1:00

Your Role
- Video continues

Reference
HCP Student Manual, *Rescue Breathing*

Resources
- AV equipment

Student Role
- Watch video

Student Objectives
- Know how to do rescue breathing for adults, children, and infants

© 2011 American Heart Association

HCP-R
22

Mouth-to-Mouth Breaths for Victims 1 Year of Age and Older

0:00 → 1:00

Your Role
- Video continues

Reference
HCP Student Manual, *Mouth-to-Mouth Breaths*

Resources
- AV equipment

Student Role
- Watch video

Student Objectives
- Know how to give mouth-to-mouth breaths for victims 1 year of age and older

© 2011 American Heart Association

OPTIONAL

HCP-R

23

Adult/Child Choking
(Responsive)
(Video Intro)

0:00 → 1:00

Your Role
- Video continues
- All students can rotate through optional practice
- If optional practice is conducted, guide student through hand placement
- Instructor will need to manually pause video for optional practice

Resources
- AV equipment
- Adult manikins

Student Role
- Optional practice

Student Objectives
- Show how to relieve choking in victims 1 year of age and older

Reference
HCP Student Manual, *Relief of Choking in Victims 1 Year of Age and Older*

© 2011 American Heart Association

HCP-R
24

Adult/Child Choking (Unresponsive)

0:00 → 1:00

Resources
- AV equipment

Student Role
- Watch video

Student Objectives
- Know to activate the emergency response system once a choking victim becomes unresponsive
- Know to start CPR if a choking adult or child becomes unresponsive

Your Role
- Video continues
- This is only a video demonstration, with no student practice

Reference
HCP Student Manual, *Relief of Choking in Victims 1 Year of Age and Older*

© 2011 American Heart Association

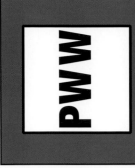

PWW

HCP-R
25A

Infant Choking
(Responsive)

0:00 → 6:00

Your Role
- Show video
- Students practice relieving choking by using back slaps and chest thrusts
- All students rotate through practice

Reference
HCP Student Manual, *Relief of Choking in Infants*

Resources
- AV equipment
- Infant manikins

Student Role
- Practice while watching video

Student Objectives
- Identify the signs of choking in a responsive infant
- Show how to relieve choking in a responsive infant

© 2011 American Heart Association

HCP-R
25B

Infant Choking (Responsive) Practice Session Details

Students practice correct technique for back slaps and chest thrusts on infant manikin

Carefully observe each student

Give corrective feedback

Make sure students use correct technique

© 2011 American Heart Association

Infant Choking (Unresponsive)

0:00 → 1:00

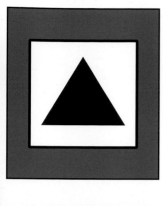

Resources
- AV equipment

Student Role
- Watch video

Student Objectives
- Know to activate the emergency response system once a choking infant becomes unresponsive
- Know to start CPR if a choking infant becomes unresponsive

Your Role
- Video continues

Reference
HCP Student Manual, *Relief of Choking in Infants*

© 2011 American Heart Association

HCP-R
27
Course Summary and Closure

0:00 → 2:00

Your Role
- Video continues
- Stop video

Reference

None

Resources
- AV equipment

Student Role
- Watch video

Student Objectives
- None

© 2011 American Heart Association

T

HCP-R
28A

28 29/30

Written Test

0:00 →

25:00

Your Role

- Divide students into 2 groups: half do written test (Lesson 28) and half do skills test (Lessons 29 and 30); then groups switch
- Distribute answer sheets
- Pass out tests
- Tell students to answer questions
- Ask students not to write on tests
- Collect tests
- Grade tests
- Pass out course evaluation forms
- Tell students to complete evaluation forms
- Collect completed evaluation forms

Resources

- Tests
- Pencils
- Answer sheets
- Course evaluation forms (print from Instructor Network)

Student Role

- Take test
- Complete course evaluation form

Student Objectives

- Show mastery of cognitive information

© 2011 American Heart Association

HCP-R

28B

Written Test Details

The written test is a closed-book test

Students may not cooperate or talk to each other during the test

When student completes the test, grade the test

Answer any questions

Students who scored <84% need immediate remediation:

- Make sure students understand errors and correct answers

- Provide remediation by giving second test or by having students verbally go over each item they got incorrect, showing understanding of incorrect items

© 2011 American Heart Association

HCP-R
29A

28 29/30

0:00

↓

30:00

1- and 2-Rescuer
Adult BLS With AED
Skills Test

Your Role

- Rotate among all students, each practicing being one of 2 rescuers performing all steps of CPR and using the AED
- Tell each student to instruct someone to activate the emergency response system and get the AED
- Carefully observe each student using the AED
- SKILLS TEST: Evaluate students' competency in 2-rescuer CPR with bag-mask
- Check off each skill as student demonstrates competency
- Emphasize following AED prompts

Reference

HCP Instructor Manual, 1- and 2-Rescuer Adult BLS With AED Skills Testing Sheet Criteria

Resources

- AV equipment
- Adult manikins
- AED trainers
- AED supplies
- Pocket masks
- Bag-masks
- One-way valves
- Stopwatches

Student Role

- Watch video
- Demonstrate full sequence of CPR with AED

Student Objectives

- Show how to use an AED with all steps of 2-rescuer CPR
- Show competency in each skill of 2-rescuer CPR and AED

© 2011 American Heart Association

1- and 2-Rescuer
Adult BLS With AED
Skills Test Details

Rotations

<u>3:1 Student-to-Manikin Ratio</u>

1st Rotation: S2 starts CPR, S1 brings and uses AED, both do CPR; S1 is tested on AED and team compressions, S2 is tested on 1-rescuer CPR and bag-mask

2nd Rotation: S3 starts CPR, S2 brings and uses AED, both do CPR; S2 is tested on AED and team compressions, S3 is tested on 1-rescuer CPR and bag-mask

3rd Rotation: S1 starts CPR, S3 brings and uses AED, both do CPR; S3 is tested on AED and team compressions, S1 is tested on 1-rescuer CPR and bag-mask

<u>2:1 Student-to-Manikin Ratio</u>

1st Rotation: S2 starts CPR, S1 brings and uses AED, both do CPR; S1 is tested on AED and team compressions, S2 is tested on 1-rescuer CPR and bag-mask

2nd Rotation: S1 starts CPR, S2 brings and uses AED, both do CPR; S2 is tested on AED and team compressions, S1 is tested on 1-rescuer CPR and bag-mask

<u>1:1 Student-to-Manikin Ratio</u>

Rotation: Two students combine as per 2:1

© 2011 American Heart Association

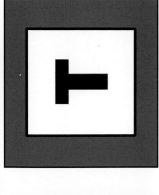

HCP-R
30A

28 29/30

0:00 → 30:00

1- and 2-Rescuer
Infant BLS
Skills Test

Your Role

- Rotate among all students, each practicing being one of 2 rescuers performing all steps of CPR
- Tell each student to tell someone to activate the emergency response system
- SKILLS TEST: Evaluate students' competency in 1- and 2-rescuer CPR with bag-mask
- Check off each skill as student demonstrates competency
- Refer student for remediation if unsuccessful on test

Resources

- AV equipment
- Infant manikins
- Pocket masks
- Bag-masks
- One-way valves
- Stopwatches

Student Role

- Demonstrate full sequence of CPR

Student Objectives

- Show how to perform 1- and 2-rescuer CPR
- Take test on each skill

Reference

HCP Instructor Manual, *1- and 2-Rescuer Infant BLS Skills Testing Sheet Criteria*

© 2011 American Heart Association

1- and 2-Rescuer
Infant BLS
Skills Test Details

Rotations

Student starts CPR and does 2 cycles; student is tested in 1-rescuer CPR (with pocket mask for breathing)

Another student comes in as 2nd rescuer, takes over breathing with bag-mask

First student continues 2-rescuer CPR as compressor for 2 cycles, then switches, takes over bag-mask breathing for 2 cycles; student is tested in 2-rescuer CPR

<u>3:1 Student-to-Manikin Ratio</u>

1st Rotation: S1 starts CPR, S2 is 2nd rescuer;   S1 is tested

2nd Rotation: S2 starts CPR, S3 is 2nd rescuer;   S2 is tested

3rd Rotation: S3 starts CPR, S1 is 2nd rescuer;   S3 is tested

<u>2:1 Student-to-Manikin Ratio</u>

1st Rotation: S1 starts CPR, S2 is 2nd rescuer;   S1 is tested

2nd Rotation: S2 starts CPR, S1 is 2nd rescuer;   S2 is tested

<u>1:1 Student-to-Manikin Ratio</u>

Rotation: Two students combine as per 2:1

© 2011 American Heart Association